Assessing the Monitoring and Evaluation Systems of IFC and MIGA

Biennial Report on Operations Evaluation

IEG WORLD BANK | IFC | MIGA
INDEPENDENT EVALUATION GROUP

Assessing the Monitoring and Evaluation Systems of IFC and MIGA

Biennial Report on Operations Evaluation

ISBN (paper): 978-0-8213-9918-7
ISBN (electronic): 978-0-8213-9919-4
DOI: 10.1596/978-0-8213-9918-7

Cover image: ©Images.com/Corbis

Library of Congress Cataloging-in-Publication Data
Biennial report on operations evaluation : assessing the monitoring and evaluation systems of IFC and MIGA.
   pages cm
   ISBN 978-0-8213-9918-7 — ISBN 978-0-8213-9919-4 (ebk)
   1. International Finance Corporation. 2. Multilateral Investment Guarantee Agency. 3. Economic development. I. World Bank.
   HG3881.5.I56B54 2013
   332.1'53—dc23
                                    2013024211

Contents

TABLES

Abbreviations

AMR	Annual Monitoring Report (IFC and MIGA)
ASOP	Advisory Services Operations Portal (IFC)
BROE	Biennial Report on Operations Evaluation
CASCR	Country Assistance Strategy Completion Report
CDI	Development Impact Department (IFC)
CRR	Credit Risk Rating system (IFC)
CV	Cannot verify (rating)
DEIS	Development Effectiveness Indicator System (MIGA)
DFI	Development finance institution
DOTS	Development Outcome Tracking System
E&S	Environmental and social
ECG	Evaluation Cooperation Group
ESRD	Environmental and Social Review Document
IDA	International Development Association
IDG	IFC Development Goals
IEG	Independent Evaluation Group
IFC	International Finance Corporation
M&E	Monitoring and evaluation
MAS	Manufacturing, agribusiness and services
MDB	Multilateral development bank
MIGA	Multilateral Investment Guarantee Agency
MSME	Micro, small, and medium-size enterprise
PCR	Project Completion Report
PER	Project Evaluation Report (IFC)
PPP	Public-private partnership
PSD	Private sector development
PSR	Project Supervision Report (IFC)
SAS	Screening, appraisal, and structuring stage
SME	Small and medium-size enterprise
TETJ	Too early to judge (rating)
XPSR	Expanded Project Supervision Report (IFC)

Acknowledgments

The evaluation report was prepared by a team led by Hiroyuki Hatashima, under the supervision of Adesimi Freeman (Head, Macro Evaluation), Stoyan Tenev (Manager, Private Sector Evaluation), and Marvin Taylor-Dormond (Director, Private Sector Evaluation) and the direction of Caroline Heider (Director-General, Evaluation, Independent Evaluation Group).

The team included Cheikh Fall, Bruce Fitzgerald, Wolfgang Gruber, Victor Malca, Sara Mareno, Albert Martinez, Srinath Sinha, and Erkin Yalcin.

Peer reviewers were Bruce Murray (former Director General, Operations Evaluation Department, Asian Development Bank) and Fredrik Korfker (former Chief Evaluator, Evaluation Department, European Bank for Reconstruction and Development). Linda Morra (former Chief Evaluation Officer, Independent Evaluation Group) commented on the approach paper.

Management and colleagues of the Independent Evaluation Group provided helpful guidance and comments, including Marianne Anderson, Stefan Apfalter, Geeta Batra, Ana Belen Barbeito, Soniya Carvalho, Unurjargal Demberel, Asita De Silva, Sid Edelmann, Jouni Eerikainen, Jack Glen, Giuseppe Iarossi, Kelly Andrews Johnson, Marylou Kam-Cheong, Ali Khadr, Beata Lenard, Brett Libresco, Aurora Medina Siy, Aghassi Mkrtchyan, Raghavan Narayanan, Bidjan Nashat, Ketevan Nozadze, Cherian Samuel, Mark Sundberg, Stephan Wegner, and Izlem Yenice.

Heather Dittbrenner edited the report. Emelda Cudilla, Chau Diem Pham, Rosemarie Pena, and Ida Scarpino provided administrative support to the team and assisted with report production.

Overview

Overview Highlights

- The International Finance Corporation (IFC) has advanced systems to gather, analyze, and apply investment and advisory project information. It has made strides in developing, aggregating, disclosing, and strategically using its development indicators.

- The Multilateral Investment Guarantee Agency (MIGA) has made progress in upgrading its system of assessing its development performance.

- In IFC, monitoring and evaluation has contributed to improved project design, supported timely interventions during execution, and strengthened strategic focus.

- IFC's and MIGA's monitoring and evaluation systems have helped improve operations and results.

- IFC's monitoring information is timely, but at the project completion point, many Advisory Services projects cannot demonstrate outcomes or impacts because not enough time has passed for these effects to have taken place.

- There are gaps in terms of measuring private sector development for investment projects and use of relevant standard indicators in Advisory Services projects. Reliability of data can be enhanced by adding more independent verification.

- Most self-evaluation has been project focused, but there is much that could be learned by extending evaluation to cover programs and strategies.

- The systems could be improved in several aspects to make evaluation more effective and to get more value from evaluation lessons.

The development paradigm has shifted toward private investment, and the private sector has become central in development strategies. Consequently, the shares of support provided by the International Finance Corporation (IFC) and the Multilateral Investment Guarantee Agency (MIGA) have grown, rising in the past decade from 21 to 35 percent of Bank Group financing.

In line with their new priorities and growing responsibilities, IFC and MIGA have adapted and are improving their monitoring and evaluation (M&E). IFC is a leading player among private sector development (PSD) agencies in monitoring, evaluating, and disclosing its development results. It has developed systems for investments (Development Outcome Tracking System—DOTS) and an advisory projects results measurement system. Its indicators and development targets are used in corporate and departmental scorecards, in strategies, and in the IFC Development Goals (IDGs). They are embedded within business processes and are influencing internal staff incentives. IFC uses self-evaluation extensively, with oversight by the Development Impact Department (CDI); it also publishes results data in its annual report.

MIGA's M&E is constrained by its business model as a political insurance provider. The arms-length nature of its relationship with the project company also limits the scope and depth of M&E. Despite this challenge, MIGA has recently started a self-evaluation system and developed a new Development Effectiveness Indicator System. Management intends to push results measurement further.

This *Biennial Report on Operations Evaluation* is an evaluation of these systems. It takes stock of the strengths and weaknesses of the development results frameworks in place for IFC Investment Services, IFC Advisory Services, and MIGA guarantees, and determines whether they (1) provide mechanisms to generate credible, timely, and relevant information; (2) support evidence-based decision making and learning; and (3) improve the performance and results of IFC's or MIGA's activities. Where they fall short, this report offers recommendations for improvements.

Credibility, Timeliness, and Relevance of M&E Information

M&E Systems for IFC Investment Projects. IFC uses DOTS to monitor the development results of its investments from screening and appraisal until closure. DOTS contains standard indicators to aggregate results and compare them across regions and industries. Investment staff fill in baseline, target, and timeline information for each indicator. The indicators are updated annually and are rated against targets in four dimensions – financial, economic, environment and social, and PSD—and IFC additionality of projects. More than 300 indicators are in use, but the Independent Evaluation Group (IEG) has found gaps in the use of indicators for PSD, which is IFC's key mandate. There seems to be a trade-off between standardization of indicators, which allow for aggregation at the corporate level, and relevance—42 percent of staff reported that there were many instances where the mandatory indicators for DOTS were not sufficient to represent the project's expected development impact.

Furthermore, information is limited on results for end beneficiaries of IFC's financial sector projects. In practice, DOTS tracking is based on "proxy" figures from the financial institutions' portfolio, such as number of loans given to a targeted business segment and the quality of that portfolio. IFC has limited knowledge about the underlying results on its end beneficiaries, and any claims would be difficult to attribute to the IFC intervention. IFC has attempted to narrow the gaps recently by completing studies on small and medium-size enterprise loans and conducting project-level assessments.

The data are timely and to a substantial extent relevant. Most data are supplied by clients, and where they are derived from audited financial statements they are of high quality. IFC has an annual data quality review cycle, but some indicators were just estimates and these were not verified at the source. The review of the annual report's external assurance was focused on data integrity and quality control process within IFC and did not contact clients or parties outside IFC to validate the data received.

IFC uses Expanded Project Supervision Reports (XPSRs) for self-evaluation of a representative sample of mature investments. IEG independently reviews the XPSRs. Their quality traditionally has been high but has deteriorated significantly over the past two years.

M&E Systems for IFC Advisory Services Projects. IFC's Advisory Services provide advice, problem solving, and training to companies and governments. They grew more than tenfold in expenditures and sixfold in staffing between FY01 and FY12. The M&E system is embedded in the project cycle from design to completion in a new information technology platform (Advisory Services Operations Portal). A logical framework model guides project design, and each business line has a standard framework with indicators for outputs, outcomes, and impacts. It is updated with semiannual supervision reports, and projects are evaluated in a final Project Completion Report (PCR). There are results measurement officers in each business line and in the regions who have strong roles throughout the project cycle. There are three levels of data quality control: project officers, results measurement officers, and CDI staff.

In FY10, Advisory Services reformed its financial management to strengthen client commitment to implementing advice and to better ensure that any subsidies are warranted based on the degree of public benefits they will realize. IEG found that the financial system faced challenges. In particular, for projects closed between 2008 and 2010, the system did not indicate the clients' in-kind contributions or parallel contributions, so it was difficult to verify actual client contributions against the original budgets as a part of evaluation of project efficiency.

PCRs are Advisory Services' instrument for self-evaluation for all closed projects. They assign ratings that are independently reviewed by IEG. Based on a review of PCRs for projects closed between 2008 and 10, IEG has found that the quality of PCRs has been improving, as they contained appropriate baseline data and useful and structured lessons. These have sharply increased the number of lessons that can be applied to future operations.

The presence of qualified results measurement specialists in the field offices also helped the quality improvement. But the same review indicated challenges in assessing outcome and impact—for many projects it was premature to judge their outcomes that could not be observed at the time of project completion and impossible to project accurately the medium- to long-term effects. One reason for gaps in capturing outcomes and impacts was the establishment of objectives that are not achievable by the time of project closure. Since FY10, Advisory Services has revised its project objective setting approach to determine what is achievable within the project's timeframe and budget, and stated that it will aim to capture intermediate results of projects. Furthermore, IFC has been conducting some selected evaluations on projects or groups of projects postcompletion, although they are not systematically conducted and not reviewed or validated by IEG.

MIGA's Development Data Gathering. MIGA is constrained by the fact that its business model is based on an arms-length relationship with the project company, and access to project information is not automatic. Nevertheless, there are new activities that indicate a more active role in measuring development results. MIGA adopted a monitoring strategy in 2011 limited to tracking compliance to MIGA's environmental and social performance standards. MIGA uses environmental and social performance standards and guidelines similar to IFC's. The applicable environmental and social (E&S) requirements are explicitly stated in every MIGA Contract of Guarantee along with the E&S reports that must be submitted to MIGA. In the same year, MIGA introduced the Development Effectiveness Indicator System to collect sector-specific indicators and six standard development impacts indicators for each project. Project data are collected twice—at the time of underwriting and three years after a project enters the portfolio—but it is premature to evaluate the effectiveness of the system for this report because only ex ante data have been collected to date and the system is still in its early stages.

MIGA Self-Evaluation. Prior to 2010, IEG conducted independent development outcome evaluations of MIGA projects. In 2010, MIGA's operational staff began self-evaluations with an emphasis on learning, and so far has conducted 17 self-evaluations. IEG found that the self-evaluation program has been useful for staff, giving them better understanding of projects' development impacts and knowledge of MIGA's policies and procedures. Active participation by MIGA underwriters, economists, and E&S specialists in self-evaluation with project site visits and stakeholder consultations, though costly, has provided an effective platform for learning. There is scope to improve the program design to increase knowledge about results and derive lessons. Also, the program's coverage is not sufficient to accurately assess MIGA's overall performance. Since the initial cost of establishing and implementing the system was high, MIGA is working with IEG to identify ways to reduce cost per project and streamline self-evaluation. MIGA has also strengthened corporate-level monitoring and reporting by introducing a set of key performance indicators reported on quarterly to the corporate executives since 2009.

Support for Evidence-Based Decision Making and Learning

This evaluation comes at a time of growing focus of IFC on development results: building a shared corporate understanding of what they are; strengthening the results measurement systems; and improving feedback into strategies and operations. The new IDGs prioritize select reach indicators of development results tracking tools for both investment and advisory services to assess progress against targets, and the M&E system is integrating various tracking mechanisms (such as credit risk and environmental and social compliance) into a results management system.

IFC's results measurement system incorporates "reach indicators" that measure the number of people reached by IFC clients or the dollar benefits to particular stakeholders, regardless of IFC's investment size. IFC's Development Goals (IDGs), which specify institutional targets for benefits or other tangible outcomes, are built on reach indicators. It is important to note that reach indicators relate to

IFC's client activities and cannot be attributed solely to IFC. Moreover, they do not capture incremental benefits compared to the situation without IFC's intervention. Given the strong emphasis on IDGs in IFC's business decisions, there is a risk that they lead to misalignment of incentives. For example, although it is too early to evaluate any changes in behavior, staff might focus on measuring large reach numbers for IDGs rather than paying attention to delivering meaningful impact that IFC projects could bring to people and society.

Monitoring for strategies' implementation has been evolving, with greater standardization of indicators to enable aggregation of development results. Development results ratings from DOTS and CDI-assigned Advisory Services PCRs are the main indicators for development outcomes, and there is growing use of reach indictors to measure progress. IFC has generally adjusted its strategies when indicators have shown that performance was lagging. Some strategies incorporate lessons from M&E and results from external evaluations. There are some important strategic areas that do not have overarching reach or outcome indicators, such as promoting competitive markets and competitiveness. Because of the growing importance of initiatives, strategies, and programmatic approaches, IFC has conducted some sector and thematic evaluations to derive lessons to guide future strategic choices; but these have not been conducted in a systematic way, and introduction of an evaluation policy would contribute to enhanced selectivity of sector and thematic evaluations.

Integrating Investment Services and Advisory Services has been a frequent component of strategies as articulated in the form of joint Investment and Advisory Services initiatives stated in IFC investment board reports. Advisory Services have been intended to unlock market potential, enabling entry of IFC and private investment and enhancing the sustainability and development impact of IFC investments. There are similarities in the two M&E systems for Investment and Advisory Services projects; however, there are many differences that could be obstacles to sharing information and operational lessons that could be relevant for both types of activities, including in linked Investment and Advisory Services projects. Moreover, harmonization of indicators between the two M&E systems would enhance close collaboration and enhance complementarities.

In addition, the learning effects of XPSRs are not fully utilized. After recent changes in the format of project approval documents—dropping the section on lessons—lessons may not be adequately considered going forward. Based on a review of XPSRs, IEG has found that recognizing and acting on lessons can improve project selection and structuring. In a sample of unsuccessful projects, existing lessons related to the factors that contributed to the failure were overlooked in the early review process; even when lessons were identified, they were not factored into project appraisal and structuring.

MIGA has progressively scaled up its self-evaluation of development results of guarantee projects since FY10 and the system is now mainstreamed. A self-evaluation is performed by senior operational staff who also prepare other new projects, so it is expected that evaluation lessons will be internalized and will influence future projects and the quality of underwriting. In a survey of MIGA staff with experience of self-evaluations, more than 70 percent responded that they improved their understanding of development impacts.

Impacts on Project Quality and Development Outcomes

M&E is expected to improve IFC's investment and advisory project results. This should occur through better project design, timely and appropriate interventions during implementation, and better strategic focus. Regression analysis based on IEG's investment project evaluations found that high-quality screening, appraisal, and structuring work that includes using lessons from evaluations mitigated high-risk elements such as sponsor risk and delivered positive development outcomes. This suggests that it is worthwhile to take risks for better results, conditional on IFC learning from its evaluative lessons—both of successes and of failures—but appropriate actions at the appraisal/screening stage should be undertaken to recognize and anticipate these risks.

M&E influences an advisory project's outcome by providing (1) a roadmap—clear objectives, baseline data, and relevant indicators—for a project to achieve its results and (2) an instrument for corrective actions during execution. Regression analysis of data for 202 advisory PCRs suggests that M&E has worked through both of these mechanisms—better design and more effective implementation have led to better outcomes.

In MIGA, self-evaluation has had its principal benefits through staff learning. But evaluation experience has also helped in updating MIGA's Underwriting Guidelines to ensure consistency and improve due diligence.

Efficiency of M&E systems

IFC spends about $14 million per year for core M&E activities with about $8,000 per Investment project and about $9,400 per Advisory Services project. The costs of M&E per investment project are a relatively low share of project processing costs. The costs per advisory project are significantly higher, but this is because the M&E is the primary source of performance tracking for advisory business and the system is relatively new so that IFC had to invest in setting up the entire system—for investment projects, performance monitoring is also carried out through investment portfolio review functions.

Although the share of M&E costs in MIGA's budget is in line with or below comparators, the cost per evaluation is estimated at $40,000, because of senior staff participation in MIGA self-evaluations. The lack of periodic tracking of project performance also requires field data collection and stakeholder interviews at the time of evaluation, which has cost implications.

Finally, the emphasis on learning by involving MIGA operational staff in undertaking self-evaluation means that its capacity to conduct a large number of self-evaluations is constrained. Because many staff have now been exposed to self-evaluation, it is anticipated that the cost per evaluation will decrease. Nevertheless, a critical challenge for MIGA's evolving M&E system—to expand coverage while reducing significantly the unit cost per evaluation—remains. This requires finding a cost-effective way of measuring the development effectiveness of MIGA projects that is consistent with MIGA's business model as a political risk insurer.

The efficiency of IFC and MIGA M&E systems appears reasonable—the total spending is 2.5 percent of administrative budget for IFC and about 1 percent for MIGA. As an illustration, for IFC, the M&E expenditures can be recouped by a very minor effect on average return on investments through the influence of M&E information on IFC's work quality and ultimately on development results and IFC's financial returns. Better equity returns for IFC through higher work quality can easily justify M&E expenditures.

Conclusion and Recommendations

IFC and MIGA have increased their emphasis on measuring and assessing their contributions to economic development and, overall, their M&E systems are becoming better equipped to inform decision making for greater development impact. In the case of IFC's Investment and Advisory Services, M&E seems to be contributing to better project results by improving project design, aiding in timely and appropriate interventions during project implementation, and strengthening the strategic focus. IEG has a series of recommendations for IFC and MIGA to make further improvements.

In light of these findings, IEG has three recommendations to improve the quality of M&E for Investment Services projects:

Where there are specific PSD objectives for investment projects, at least one relevant PSD indicator should be systematically tracked in the DOTS. PSD such as improved competition, demonstration effects of a business model, or host country sectoral transformations—is a rationale for many IFC investments. However, in the investment projects' DOTS, only a few indicators track PSD and about 46 percent of projects sampled had no such indicator. In the sample, only 28 percent of evaluated projects had DOTS indicators that were directly relevant to the expected PSD outcomes such as demonstration effects or increased competition that are critical for IFC's development mandate. There is a need for systematic reflection of expected PSD effects of IFC investment interventions, including causal chains to link IFC's activities to outcomes and indicators.

All XPSRs should be delivered on time and their quality improved through better management oversight, guidance, and clearance, plus the involvement of senior investment officers in conducting XPSRs. The quality of XPSRs has declined by three measures: (1) XPSR's rated as "good practice" dropped from 50 to 25 percent between 2007 and 2011; (2) in 2011, staff assigned higher self-ratings for development outcome and IFC work quality in 20 percent and 18 percent of XPSRs, respectively, as compared with independent assessments, and the gaps between the self and IEG ratings have been increasing in the last four years; (3) for the first time in 2010 IFC did not complete six XPSRs during the program year. Possible reasons are (1) less experienced junior staff drafting self-evaluations without sufficient oversight, (2) a larger XPSR program following IFC's portfolio growth over the last five years, or (3) portfolio staff also working on new projects, which takes precedence. IEG recommends that management work to restore the quality of the XPSR program.

IFC should conduct selective tests and reviews to validate information provided by clients. For unaudited information, selective direct data verification is needed to enhance the credibility and reliability of data supplied by companies. Any assumptions and data limitations or biases should be publicly disclosed. The external assurance provider's mandate should be expanded to include assessment of the credibility and attribution of data—particularly related to IDGs—appropriate verification, and whether IFC is effectively disclosing data limitations or biases. DOTS indicators are based in part on data from audited financial reports, company annual reports, and other validated sources. However, other data are based on assumptions by client and IFC staff, and IFC does not have a process to verify data integrity other than through a desk review of information received. IFC has pioneered external assurance of its development results reporting. However, this review has been limited to a small portion of the information; only ex post micro, small, and medium enterprises loan data are externally assured—that is, only 1 of 15 measures of Development Reach by IFC investment clients. Moreover, similar to IFC's internal CDI quality control, the assurance provider's review does not include contacting clients, visiting projects, or communicating with field-based staff. Direct data verification for some data that are based on less credible sources would enhance the credibility and reliability of data supplied by companies and staff, and any assumptions and data limitations or biases should be publicly disclosed.

Furthermore, IEG has one recommendation to make the M&E information more valuable in investment decision making and learning:

Reinforce the culture of learning lessons from IFC's previous investment projects during appraisal, design, structuring, and approval stages. Reintroducing the lessons section in appraisal documents may contribute to this. IEG recommends that the lessons learned from prior projects be used in project appraisal and structuring discussions. It would also be helpful to provide guidance for identifying lessons and reflecting lessons for meaningful discussion during the review stage. Many factors affect investment project outcomes, but evaluation results have shown that projects with poor outcomes are associated with poor up-front work quality, which includes ignoring lessons. The lessons serve as a basis for defining the areas of focus during appraisal. IFC had a section in its project documentation to list the salient lessons, but the section was recently dropped.

Two recommendations to improve quality of M&E system for Advisory Services follow:

Revise the standard indicators based on appropriate results chains or theory of change of business lines, strategies, and project objectives. Among PCRs completed in 2010, 90 percent fell short of using relevant standard indicators. Standard indicators in Advisory Services are not always adequate to track project results as per project objectives. In some cases, poor core indicators linked to poorly articulated objectives have led to weak impact measurement. Moreover, the increasing reliance on standard indicators that are only weakly related to project objectives could transform the self-evaluation process into a monitoring exercise focused on checking achievement of standard indicators rather than analyzing achievement of objectives and understanding the factors behind success or failure.

Address the issue of timing of IFC's Advisory Services self-evaluation system to ensure projects are sufficiently mature to more meaningfully assess their development results. In doing so, IFC might either consider conducting self-evaluation two to three years post completion, possibly on a sample of projects as done for XPSRs, or launching a post-completion system based on clear selection criteria for projects to be included.

IEG could not assign development effectiveness ratings to 18 percent of projects selected for evaluation, in most instances (65 percent of the cases) because projects had not achieved results at the time of IEG evaluation and, in 35 percent of instances, because of insufficient information and lack of credible evidence. Moreover, even among those projects for which IEG assigned development effectiveness ratings, 41 percent could not be rated at the impact level because impacts had not been achieved by evaluation/project closure or because there was insufficient information and evidence to assign a rating.

Given the limitations of the PCR instrument to adequately assess outcomes and impacts at project closure, IFC may not count on sufficient evidence to systematically evaluate completed advisory services projects and provide insights into the causal relationships between interventions and longer-term results. IFC has attempted to capture longer-term results through impact and other types of evaluations as well as through some ad hoc post completion monitoring efforts. However, this has not been done in a systematic way across IFC and is largely de-linked from IFC's self-evaluation system. Since FY10, Advisory Services has revised its project objective-setting approach to determine what is achievable within the project timeframe and budget, and stated that they are aiming to capture intermediate results of projects. This practice may be strengthened and supplemented by a systematic, sample-based postcompletion evaluation system, aimed at capturing impacts.

IEG has one recommendation to make the M&E information more valuable in Advisory Services decision making and learning:

In the current process of revising PCR guidelines, IFC should include an assessment of IFC work quality in Advisory Services self-evaluations. The PCR framework does not contain a direct assessment of IFC's quality of work. The section of IFC's role and contribution usually includes some aspects of self-evaluation of IFC's role, but not systematically. Based on the experience from XPSRs (which includes this section), IFC would get greater learning benefits by explicitly evaluating the quality of its work—design and execution—and its relationship to other performance dimensions. IFC may consider introducing the work quality dimension in a revised version of the PCR guidelines. This would help align the evaluation frameworks for Investment Services and Advisory Services.

IEG has two recommendations to make the M&E information more valuable in decision making and learning at the corporate level:

When IFC interventions involve combined Investment and Advisory Services, project M&E should more explicitly reflect results measurement of both advisory business lines and industries. IFC is increasingly combining Investment and Advisory Services to achieve development goals. Some of the lessons in Investment projects could be relevant to Advisory Services and vice versa. Although there are some common elements in the respective results measurement frameworks, there are also asymmetries.

IFC's regional, country, industry sector, and Advisory Services business line strategies and initiatives should contain an explicit results matrix to assess strategic objectives, with relevant indicators to track progress and evaluate in a systematic manner, preferably embedded in periodic strategy updates. IFC should pilot approaches to improve the measuring and reporting of key results on the areas of critical institutional objectives that go beyond project performance, such as private sector development and poverty reduction. Despite the growing importance of initiatives, strategies, and programmatic approaches, IFC has not systematically evaluated such strategic interventions. Most evaluations are conducted at the project level, which are not, by themselves, sufficient to measure strategic impact on sector efficiency, market functioning, competitiveness, or poverty reduction.

IEG has one recommendation to improve MIGA's M&E system:

MIGA should:

- *Streamline the project-evaluation approach and process to align more closely with MIGA's business model and conditions on data gathering.*
- *Reduce the cost burden on project evaluation, possibly by strengthening periodic collection of project data in line with industry practices.*
- *Increase coverage of evaluated projects in order to enhance the ability to derive meaningful results at the corporate level.*

MIGA has mainstreamed self-evaluation of its guarantees and has strengthened some aspects of its project monitoring. However, the coverage of MIGA projects through self-evaluation can be strengthened to enhance the ability to assess MIGA's overall development performance. As a development institution, MIGA should be able to know the development effectiveness of its portfolio.

Management Response

I. Introduction

Management welcomes the Independent Evaluation Group's (IEG) *Biennial Report on Operations Evaluation* (BROE), which assesses the monitoring and evaluation systems (M&E) of the International Finance Corporation (IFC) and the Multilateral Investment Guarantee Agency (MIGA). M&E plays an important role in understanding and enhancing our development impact, and we value IEG's contribution in this regard. The report comes at an opportune time, given further enhancements in IFC's M&E systems since the last BROE on IFC in 2008.

This note has a separate section for the IFC Management Response and for the MIGA Management Response. The specific IFC and MIGA response to the report's recommendations are in the Management Action Record matrix.

II. IFC Management Response

We are pleased that the report recognizes that IFC continues to be in the lead on M&E among private sector–oriented development finance institutions (DFIs). This is welcome confirmation that IFC has its priorities right on M&E and that the enhancements in our frameworks and systems are best practice. We believe we have made significant progress in developing, aggregating, disclosing, and using development results to formulate strategy and improve operations.

RECENT M&E INITIATIVES IN IFC

IFC has allocated extensive resources in continuing to improve development results measurement, to achieve greater impact. Since the 2008 BROE, IFC has pioneered the use of quantitative thematic development targets to drive strategy and operations by piloting, testing, and implementing IFC Development Goals (IDGs); two IDGs became operational in FY13, and three more are scheduled to do the same in FY14.

Since the 2008 BROE, IFC has been implementing its new self-evaluation strategy to complement IEG's independent evaluations, working with operational departments to learn from past performance to inform strategy and enhance future operations. We are pleased that IEG acknowledges IFC's sectoral and thematic evaluations, which typically cover multiple regions and priority areas of our business. For example, in FY13 we completed a global evaluation covering select activities of the business regulation product in the investment climate business line, which included 59 projects across six regions; we also finished a housing finance evaluation that compared results across more and less-successful case studies in South Asia and Latin America.

In addition to evaluation, IFC conducts programmatic studies to develop new methodologies and inform our strategic approach on specific cross-cutting themes, including the IFC job study, the China review of finance-related IFC operations, the global demonstration effects study, and the global public private partnerships gender study. Moving forward, IFC will ensure that its annual self-evaluation and research work program continues to go beyond project-level performance and will explicitly track work dedicated to these activities to establish a baseline and track progress over time.

IFC has also played a leadership role in an initiative to harmonize private sector development impact indicators of various DFIs. IFC took the lead in convening DFIs on this issue, proposed hiring an external consulting firm that would benchmark all our standard investment services indicators and make best practice recommendations to participating DFIs by an established delivery date. The objective was to adopt a set of common core indicators, which would lower shared clients' reporting costs and facilitate learning among DFIs. In 2012, more than 20 DFIs agreed to the proposal and together finalized terms of reference for a competitive selection of a consulting firm that is currently reviewing indicators and about to make recommendations to the group of participating DFIs.

IFC has also established a global Results Measurement Network of more than 60 staff who work full time on results measurement, as well as many of the part-time Development Outcome Tracking System (DOTS) champions. This has formalized the M&E career stream in IFC, with three important consequences: it is improving results frameworks at the operational level; it is fostering knowledge sharing of good practice among M&E professionals in IFC; and it is creating more opportunities for professional advancement.

There are several ongoing efforts that will further improve IFC's M&E. As a follow-on to the recently completed jobs study, IFC is developing an implementation support plan, which should increase the job creation effects of our operational activities. IFC has recently undertaken a demonstration effects study, designed to help us better understand the factors associated with greater levels of demonstration effects, with the intention of feeding that learning back into strategy and project design. Finally, we have also initiated a study of projects considered as transformational; the objective is to identify characteristics of transformational projects from current work, so we can design those features into future projects and track progress.

COMMENTS ON THE REPORT

IEG has downgraded "best practice" Expanded Project Supervision Reports (XPSRs) across the board. IEG's individual Evaluation Notes (EvNotes) used to flag those XPSRs that contain superior evaluative documentation, analysis, and judgment as "best practice." IFC has then used this "best practice" XPSR recognition as an input to some performance awards program. However, the BROE reclassified "best practice" to "good practice," with the apparent implication that other XPSRs are not good. This has caused significant confusion. Going forward, IFC remains committed to delivering high-quality XPSRs, and we appreciate our partnership with IEG on this matter. We would like to work with IEG on a training program for investment officers on how to write high-quality XPSRs, including clarity on the way in which IEG decides whether an XPSR is good practice or not. We also look forward to a more timely completion IEG EvNotes; we have observed several instances where the lag time between the staff XPSR and the subsequent IEG EvNote has contributed to different ratings.

On Advisory Services, management notes that the report covered projects completed in the period FY08–10, which coincided with a period of significant internal consolidation and reform, as well as early effects of the global financial crisis. Since FY10, we have continued to introduce reforms to project design and project evaluations and to sharpen strategic focus. Project Completion Reports (PCRs) show that development effectiveness ratings have improved consistently over the past few years, reaching 72 percent in 2011.

Unlike the 2008 BROE, this report does not include IEG's self-evaluation of its M&E framework. This is unfortunate, as IFC's M&E systems are influenced and complemented by those of IEG. For example, the XPSR and the PCR systems were developed by IEG, and there are extensive interactions between IFC and IEG before an annual program is completed. IFC management believes that re-introducing IEG's self-evaluation in future BROEs would permit a more complete discussion and potentially help improve the interrelated process between IFC and IEG.

CONCLUSION

Our differences on some areas of the BROE do not dilute the overall value of the report to management. IEG plays an important complementary role within IFC's M&E system. The report is a good example of the substantial contribution IEG makes to enhancing IFC's development impact.

III. MIGA Management Response

MIGA thanks IEG for this constructive and insightful evaluation. This report is very timely, as MIGA is mounting a concerted effort to move our M&E activities to the next level to strengthen the feedback loop to operational learning and project design. The report will be useful in a number of important respects including actions/progress made recently in starting up and mainstreaming MIGA's self-evaluation program, scaling up environmental and social (E&S) monitoring, and implementing portfolio-wide development outcome tracking (Development Effectiveness Indicator System).

The report mentions up front that, given where MIGA stands in terms of developing its M&E system, it is "too early for a definitive evaluation." Thus, the report's conclusions and recommendations should be seen as preliminary and evolving over time.

The report accurately acknowledges the differences between IFC's and MIGA's business models and the challenges that MIGA inevitably faces in evaluating the projects for which it provides guarantees, given its arms-length relationship to the project enterprise. This is in distinct contrast to investors and lenders; for example, MIGA does not receive memberships on project enterprise boards of directors, which would allow for enhanced dialogue and access. The report recognizes this reality and its overarching influence on M&E systems and procedures that MIGA uses.

In the context of MIGA's business model, it would also be helpful to add that related to being at an "arms-length" distance from the project, MIGA has to be mindful of all transaction costs that are being imposed on a client. Client tolerances for the "hidden" costs of working with the World Bank Group are limited.

The report identifies relevant shortcomings in some MIGA processes, such as records management and E&S contract compliance follow-up. MIGA agrees with these findings and, as the report acknowledges, is actively working to address these.

MIGA's evaluation program in its current form (that is, since FY10) has been carefully developed, and IEG has been heavily involved in numerous aspects of this program (for example, drafting comprehensive guidelines, sampling procedures, initial training, and validation protocols). IEG is also involved in the ongoing efforts to identify ways to streamline and otherwise reduce costs of conducting MIGA's self-evaluations. The report should note IEG's involvement in helping MIGA set up an M&E system, to underscore that what we have in place has drawn on independent input.

There are some findings in the report where MIGA either has a different view or believes further context setting is necessary. These include:

- The cost of undertaking MIGA self-evaluations has come down. A few years ago we estimated it cost approximately $25,000 per evaluation excluding travel ($50,000 with travel); today the range is now $15,000–17,000, excluding travel.

- The principal cost driver is not obtaining information from the client. Rather, it is obtaining and analyzing information beyond what the client can or should provide. For example, to carry out economic rate of return analysis, MIGA must collect data such as third-party stakeholder views and relevant economic parameters for comparisons (that is, for energy projects, the marginal electricity costs).

- The cost comparisons between MIGA and IFC are misleading, given that the two institutions are in different stages of their M&E capacity building.

- The report claims that the "small number of evaluations" is a constraint to learning from evaluations. Some clarification is warranted here. Starting from zero, MIGA has progressively scaled up delivery from three to five to seven evaluations per year since FY10. Seven evaluations done well, with in-depth site visits, intensive interaction with multiple stakeholders, led by front line staff, provides more effective "learning" than would 15–20 cursory exercises.

The IEG-administered survey of MIGA staff for this report (in which 90 percent of front line staff participated) clearly bears this out.

- The report exhorts MIGA to seek cost-effective ways of reducing costs of evaluation in ways that are consistent with MIGA's business model as a political risk insurance provider. MIGA unreservedly subscribes to this and has been making considerable efforts to do so. The report acknowledges that MIGA and IEG management constituted a joint working group to address this matter in the context of the GPS4, which is to serve as a framework for the exercise.

Management Action Record

IEG Findings and Conclusions	IEG Recommendations	Acceptance by Management	Management Response
IFC Investment Services			
1. Gaps in monitoring private sector development impacts in DOTS for investment projects. Private sector development (PSD) such as improved competition, demonstration effects of a business model, or host country sectoral transformations is a rationale for many IFC investments. However, in the investment projects' DOTS, only a few indicators track PSD, and about 46 percent of projects sampled had no such indicator. In the sample, only 28 percent of evaluated projects had DOTS indicators that were directly relevant to the expected PSD outcomes, such as demonstration effects or increased competition that are critical for IFC's development mandate. There is a need for systematic reflection of expected PSD effects of IFC investment interventions, including causal chains to link IFC's activities to outcomes and indicators.	**Where there are specific PSD objectives for investment projects, at least one relevant PSD indicator should be systematically tracked in DOTS.**	Agree	PSD is the most challenging area for which to articulate outcomes. IFC is already making several efforts to improve the tracking and monitoring of PSD indicators, including: • Over the last six months, IFC undertook a demonstrations effect study—a study designed to help us better understand the factors associated with greater levels of demonstration effects—with the intention of feeding that learning back into strategy and project design. • IFC renewed efforts to harmonize indicators for investment projects with others DFIs in FY12. This opportunity will allow us to identify and apply the best PSD indicators. • The Manufacturing, Agribusiness and Services Industry Group has revamped all mandatory indicators in FY12, including PSD indicators for each subsector. IFC agrees that a better articulated PSD impact is needed—for example, the channels by which the PSD outcomes transmit to recipients beyond IFC's clients. Over FY14–15, IFC will work to clarify definitions and causal links for staff. We will also work with operational departments to map and increase the use of PSD indicators for projects with clear PSD objectives.

IEG Findings and Conclusions	IEG Recommendations	Acceptance by Management	Management Response
2. Declining quality of self-evaluation reporting (XPSR). The quality of XPSRs has declined by three measures: (1) XPSRs rated as "good practice" dropped from 50 to 25 percent between 2007 and 2011; (2) in 2011, staff assigned higher self-ratings for development outcome and IFC work quality in 20 percent and 18 percent of XPSRs, respectively, compared with independent assessments, and the gaps between the self and IEG ratings have been increasing in the last four years; and (3) for the first time in 2010 IFC did not complete six XPSRs during the program year. Possible reasons are (1) less experienced junior staff drafting self-evaluations without sufficient oversight, (2) a larger XPSR program following IFC's portfolio growth over the last five years, and (3) portfolio staff also working on new projects, which takes precedence.	**All XPSRs should be delivered on time and their quality improved through better management oversight, guidance, and clearance, plus the involvement of senior investment officers in conducting XPSRs.**	**Agree**	IEG's relabeling of best practice XPSRs to good practice has caused confusion. There is no evidence to support the assertion that 25 percent of XPSRs being considered best practice (now relabeled as good practice) is not a good achievement. The widening gap between self and IEG ratings could be a result of tougher IEG ratings over these four years, rather than "softer" self-ratings. We agree that all XPSRs should be completed and delivered on time. We also look forward to a more timely completion of all IEG's EvNotes. We agree that the likely causes of the ratings variance are (1) a larger XPSR program and (2) investment staff giving new project processing or immediate portfolio concerns precedence over XPSR completion. We propose that we work with IEG to limit the number of XPSRs per staff, without losing representativeness. This will have the added benefit of spreading the learning to more staff. In addition, we propose that we work with IEG on a training program for investment officers on how to write high-quality XPSRs, including clarity around the way in which IEG decides whether an XPSR is good practice or not.

IEG Findings and Conclusions	IEG Recommendations	Acceptance by Management	Management Response
3. Enhancing the credibility of DOTS indicators. DOTS indicators are based in part on data from audited financial reports, company annual reports, and other validated sources. However, other data are based on assumptions by client and IFC staff, and IFC does not have a process to verify data integrity other than through a desk review of information received. IFC has pioneered external assurance of its development results reporting. However, this review has been limited to a small portion of the information; only ex post verification of the information; only 1 of 15 measures of development reach by IFC investment clients. Moreover, similar to IFC's internal Development Impact Department (CDI) quality control, the assurance provider's review does not include contacting clients, visiting projects, or communicating with field-based staff. Direct data verification for some data that are based on less credible sources would enhance the credibility and reliability of data supplied by companies and staff, and any assumptions and data limitations or biases should be publicly disclosed.	**IFC should conduct selective tests and reviews to validate information provided by clients.** **For unaudited information, selective direct data verification is needed to enhance the credibility and reliability of data supplied by companies. Any assumptions and data limitations or biases should be publicly disclosed.** **The external assurance provider's mandate should be expanded to include assessment of the credibility and attribution of data—particularly related to IDGs—appropriate verification, and whether IFC is effectively disclosing data limitations or biases.**	**Agree on selective data validation** **Disagree on expanding the external assurance provider's mandate**	As the BROE report pointed out, IFC is the leader among multilateral development banks with regards to tracking and monitoring development results. IFC has continued to refine our quality review process and further strengthened the results measurement network to improve staff understanding of development impact as well as the data quality. Over the last fiscal year, IFC has conducted a pilot verification of Advisory Services outcome data quality in the Africa Region. We will incorporate lessons learned from that experience. In FY14, we will implement a similar verification process of a sample of Investment Services projects to assess any data quality issues on the investment side. We disagree with the recommendation to expand the mandate of the external assurance provider to include direct assessment of the credibility and attribution of results. We see no evidence that it is necessary, and it would be more costly to clients. We already have stringent data quality controls in place through different levels of data scrutiny including: • Portfolio officers collect and enter data into DOTS and upload the sources of information in iDesk. • DOTS champions and results measurement staff review data quality within a deadline given by CDI. CDI provides weekly updates of reach data quality focusing on year-on-year variations (large increases/decreases or no variations), big contributors, zero values, and accuracy of gender data component.

IEG Findings and Conclusions	IEG Recommendations	Acceptance by Management	Management Response
			• CDI reviews DOTS ratings and indicators quality against IFC's official guidelines as well as reach data quality. • DOTS champions request portfolio officers to make any changes and to provide any additional information that has been requested through this thorough review process. We are additionally undertaking pilot quality control tests, in FY13 and FY14, and will then determine whether we need any additional data quality controls. At that point, we will consider asking the external assurance provider to review the appropriateness of these additional control processes. We do not consider it necessary or helpful to ask the assurance provider to undertake direct assessments of the quality of the data itself—in effect, this would be a third or fourth layer of checking—which would create unnecessary additional intrusion for IFC's clients.
4. Lessons from evaluation are critical. Many factors affect investment project outcomes, but evaluation results have shown that projects with poor outcomes are associated with poor up-front work quality, which includes ignoring lessons. The lessons serve as a basis for defining the areas of focus during appraisal. IFC had a section in its project documentation to list the salient lessons, but the section was recently dropped.	**Reinforce the culture of learning lessons from IFC's previous investment projects during appraisal, design, structuring, and approval stages. Reintroducing the lessons section in appraisal documents may contribute this.** **IEG recommends that the lessons learned from prior projects be used in project appraisal and structuring discussions. It would also be helpful to provide guidance for identifying lessons and reflecting lessons for meaningful discussion during the review stage.**	Agree	We welcome this recommendation. Lessons from past operations have always been an important consideration in IFC's project due diligence process. As part of the Business Process Improvement initiatives, IFC streamlined the information presented in Project Data Sheet-Concept documentation to increase the focus on project parameters such as IFC's strategic context, additionality, development impact, and business case. This change in document format has not diminished the importance of lessons learned in informing project design. On the contrary, IFC has strengthened its team of industry specialists and introduced sector leaders in most transaction teams to further facilitate sharing of best practices and lessons learned. Sector leaders are seasoned investment staff who provide advice and share lessons of experience to transaction teams. Going forward, IFC will further promote the culture of learning by making lessons from different sources more accessible. For example, IFC is developing a knowledge strategy that is expected to enhance the creation, collection and sharing of lessons.

IEG Findings and Conclusions	IEG Recommendations	Acceptance by Management	Management Response
IFC Advisory Services			
5. Need to revisit standard indicators. Among PCRs completed in 2010, 90 percent fell short of using *relevant* standard indicators. Standard indicators in Advisory Services are not always adequate to track project results as per project objectives. In some cases, poor core indicators linked to poorly articulated objectives have led to weak impact measurement. Moreover, the increasing reliance on standard indicators that are only weakly related to project objectives could transform the self-evaluation process into a monitoring exercise focused on checking achievement of standard indicators rather than analyzing achievement of objectives and understanding the factors behind success or failure.	**Revise the standard indicators based on appropriate results chains or theory of change of business lines, strategies, and project objectives.**	Agree	Many revisions and improvements to indicators have occurred since the cohort of projects examined by IEG in this BROE: • All Advisory Services business lines revised their M&E frameworks, including standard indicators, in FY10 and FY11. • Revised approach in FY10 to ensure teams were setting realistic project objectives. • Quality at Entry review was started across all projects from FY10 to ensure linkages with objectives and indicators. Recent years' data shows improved use of standard indicators. A Working Group of Global Business Line Directors was established in 2012 to oversee a review of standard indicators. As part of this process, emphasis is being placed on aligning Advisory and Investment Services metrics wherever possible. This will take into account the results of the indicator harmonization exercise with other DFIs.

IEG Findings and Conclusions	IEG Recommendations	Acceptance by Management	Management Response
6. Capturing Advisory Services projects' outcomes and impacts. IEG could not assign development effectiveness ratings to 18 percent of projects selected for evaluation, in most instances (65 percent of the cases) because projects had not achieved results at the time of IEG evaluation and, in 35 percent of instances, because of insufficient information and lack of credible evidence. Moreover, even among those projects for which IEG assigned development effectiveness ratings, 41 percent could not be rated at the impact level because impacts had not been achieved by evaluation/project closure or because there was insufficient information and evidence to assign a rating. Given the limitations of the PCR instrument to adequately assess outcomes and impacts at project closure, IFC may not count on sufficient evidence to systematically evaluate completed advisory services projects, and provide insights into the causal relationships between interventions and longer term results. IFC has attempted to capture longer-term results through impact and other types of evaluations as well as through some ad hoc postcompletion monitoring efforts. However, this has not been done in a systematic way across IFC and is largely de-inked from IFC's self-evaluation system. Since FY10, Advisory Services has revised its project objective-setting approach to determine what is achievable within the project timeframe and budget and stated that they are aiming to capture intermediate results of projects. This practice may be strengthened and supplemented by a systematic, sample-based postcompletion evaluation system aimed at capturing impacts.	**Address the issue of timing of IFC's Advisory Services self-evaluation system to ensure projects are sufficiently mature to assess more meaningfully their development results. In doing so, IFC might either consider conducting self-evaluation two to three years postcompletion, possibly on a sample of projects, as is done for XPSRs, or launching a postcompletion system based on clear selection criteria for projects to be included.**	Agree	Amongst the many improvements to results measurement for Advisory Services activities in recent years, reforms have included measures to ensure project objectives are realistic, and at least the intermediate impacts of the projects are assessed. In tandem, management has been reviewing the array of tools it has to ensure rigorous and cost-effective evaluation of longer-term results and impacts. This includes the new IFC evaluation strategy and work toward an appropriate Advisory Services postcompletion monitoring system, which we expect to roll-out by the end of CY13.

IEG Findings and Conclusions	IEG Recommendations	Acceptance by Management	Management Response
7. Work Quality assessment in Advisory Services project evaluation. The PCR framework does not contain a direct assessment of IFC's quality of work. The section of IFC's role and contribution usually includes some aspects of self-evaluation of IFC's role but not systematically. Based on the experience from XPSRs (which includes this section), IFC would get greater learning benefits by explicitly evaluating the quality of its work—design and execution—and its relationship to other performance dimensions. IFC may consider introducing the work quality dimension in a revised version of the PCR Guidelines. This would help align the evaluation frameworks for Investment Services and Advisory Services.	**In the current process of revising PCR guidelines, IFC should include an assessment of IFC work quality in Advisory Services self-evaluations.**	Agree	As part of the current IFC-IEG review of PCR guidelines, management will consider alternative approaches to assessing work quality in advisory services projects. Subject to management and IEG agreement, the PCR guidelines should be revised by the end of CY13.
IFC Corporate-Level M&E			
8. Alignment between investment and advisory services results measurement framework. IFC is increasingly combining Investment and Advisory Services to achieve development goals. Some of the lessons in investment projects could be relevant to Advisory Services and vice versa. Although there are some common elements in the respective results measurement frameworks, there are also asymmetries.	**When IFC interventions involve combined Investment and Advisory Services, project M&E should more explicitly reflect results measurement of both business lines and industries.**	Agree	IFC is working toward more Advisory Services and Investment Services alignment in the following dimensions: • IDGs—Harmonization of indicators has already taken place for some IDGs: micro-, medium-, and small enterprise access to finance, GHGs, and infrastructure access. In addition, many joint Advisory Services-Investment Services projects have common indicators. • Harmonization—We have a sequenced plan for indicator harmonization. This starts with recommendations for Investment Services indicator harmonization with other DFIs; these recommendations will then feed into a plan to harmonize a subset of Investment and Advisory Services indicators that would be tested in FY14 and used for joint investment and advisory projects by FY15. This work will also feed into the World Bank Group Change Team working on harmonizing results frameworks across the World Bank Group.

IEG Findings and Conclusions	IEG Recommendations	Acceptance by Management	Management Response
			• Evaluation—We have increased the number of joint Advisory Services-Investment Services evaluations of projects and programs. Recent examples include Progresemos (completed), China Review (completed), Health in Africa (completed), Performance-Based Grant Initiative (ongoing), Sustainable Energy Finance Global Review (planned), and Education for Employment (planned).
9. Evaluation of IFC initiatives, strategies, and programmatic approaches. Despite the growing importance of initiatives, strategies, and programmatic approaches, IFC has not systematically evaluated such strategic interventions. Most evaluations are conducted at the project level, which are not, by themselves, sufficient to measure strategic impact on sector efficiency, market functioning, competitiveness, or poverty reduction.	**IFC's regional, country, industry sector, and Advisory Services business line strategies and initiatives should contain an explicit results matrix to assess strategic objectives, with relevant indicators to track progress and evaluate in a systematic manner, preferably embedded in periodic strategy updates.** **IFC should pilot approaches to improve the measuring and reporting of key results on the areas of critical institutional objectives that go beyond project performance, such as private sector development and poverty reduction.**	**Agree**	IFC already tracks the results of its geographic, industry, and thematic strategies at two levels: (1) the IFC corporate level and (2) the World Bank Group level. Going forward, IFC will pilot more systematic approaches to results measurement for internal IFC strategy updates/reviews. **At the corporate level:** IFC outlines its corporate strategy in the annual Road Map Paper, covering a three-year rolling period. This is a synthesis of regional, country, industry, and thematic approaches and their contributions to both IFC strategic priorities and corporate goals. It includes a Corporate Scorecard that tracks IFC's performance in each strategic focus area and corporate goal. IFC's regional, country, industry, and thematic objectives are therefore already tracked at the corporate level. IFC also undertakes on an as-needed basis an internal review/update of its strategic approaches in specific themes or geographical areas. IFC will pilot the establishment of results measurement frameworks in select internal strategy reviews/updates. These pilots will use existing IFC indicators and will consider any additional indicators that may be needed for corporate-wide or Bank Group-wide initiatives. We will refine our approach as we learn from experience.

IEG Findings and Conclusions	IEG Recommendations	Acceptance by Management	Management Response
			At the World Bank Group level: IFC participates in the formulation of formal Bank Group-wide strategies at all levels, including the results measurement frameworks for such strategies. We believe that this is an effective and efficient way of tracking IFC's formal geographic or thematic strategies.
MIGA			
10. Remaining gaps in MIGA's self-evaluation. MIGA has mainstreamed self-evaluation of its guarantees and has strengthened some aspects of its project monitoring. However, the coverage of MIGA projects through self-evaluation can be strengthened to enhance the ability to assess MIGA's overall development performance. As a development institution, MIGA should be able to know the development effectiveness of its portfolio.	**Streamline the project-evaluation approach and process to align more closely with MIGA's business model and conditions on data gathering.** **Reduce the cost burden on project evaluation, possibly by strengthening periodic collection of project data in line with industry practices.** **Increase coverage of evaluated projects in order to enhance the ability to derive meaningful results at the corporate level.**	Agree	MIGA shares the conviction that self-evaluations should be simplified and better adapted to MIGA's business model and has worked closely with IEG to identify a way to do so. Creating an evaluation approach that is appropriate to MIGA's involvement in its projects makes eminent sense. There is a MIGA-IEG working group in place that is endeavoring to simplify procedures along these lines. The work is ongoing. In terms of reducing costs, unit costs per evaluation have come down in recent years, primarily as efficiencies have increased with experience. The major changes in the cost structure, however, will be achieved with meaningful streamlining. With respect to assessing corporate-level results, MIGA's Development Effectiveness Indicator System is now in its third year and will play the important role of collecting ex post impact data on all MIGA's outstanding guarantees, thereby allowing for a portfolio level assessment of results.

Chairperson's Summary: Committee on Development Effectiveness

The Committee on Development Effectiveness considered the Independent Evaluation Group's (IEG) *Biennial Report on Operations Evaluation: Assessing the Monitoring and Evaluation Systems of IFC and MIGA* and the draft Management Response.

Summary

The Committee commended IEG's evaluation and congratulated the International Finance Corporation (IFC) and the Multilateral Investment Guarantee Agency (MIGA) for significant recent progress in their monitoring and evaluation (M&E) systems, yet emphasized that there is still more to be done. They thanked the External Expert Panel for its assessment of the evaluation, noting agreement in particular with the importance of learning to inform the design of projects and advisory services.

The Committee agreed that the evaluation's findings identify areas to further improve IFC's and MIGA's M&E systems to make them more robust and stronger in providing evidence-based data. The Committee concurred with the majority of the evaluation's recommendations, with one exception pertaining to the method IFC should use to undertake additional quality checks to validate client information, in particular for IFC investment projects. In this regard, members concurred with the steps proposed by IFC to pilot additional tests internally and to consider having the assurance provider review such tests at the completion of the pilot. In addition, members indicated the need for better articulation of additionality in project Board documents, the importance of incorporating lessons learned into project/investment design, and the need to balance coverage and costs of M&E systems. They suggested exploiting synergies between MIGA and IFC, including joint self-evaluations, and stressed the importance of enhancing data quality to ensure robust self-evaluations.

Anna Brandt, Chairperson

Statement by the External Expert Panel

Overall, the panel found the report to be of high quality. It provides timely and useful information to the managements of the International Finance Corporation (IFC) and the Multilateral Investment Guarantee Agency (MIGA) and to the Committee on Development Effectiveness. The report was comprehensive, well structured, well written, and balanced in terms of identifying both strengths and weaknesses and pointing out the progress that has been made over time and areas where further improvements are needed. The report posed appropriate evaluation questions that were well defined, presented the necessary evaluation evidence, and analyzed the information in a sound manner. The recommendations were clear and were supported by the analysis and evidence presented.

The panel believes that it is useful to have periodic independent reviews of monitoring and evaluation (M&E) systems to see what is working well, where there are gaps in coverage or weaknesses that need to be addressed, and how—or if—the M&E information is actually used in decision making. To the panel's knowledge, the Independent Evaluation Group (IEG) is the only evaluation department among the multilateral development banks (MDBs) that regularly assesses M&E systems. Past editions of the *Biennial Report on Operations Evaluation* (BROE) have contributed to the improvement of IFC's and MIGA's self-evaluation systems. In effect, IEG, IFC, and MIGA have collaborated over many years to develop and improve the organizations' M&E systems. Given the influence of past BROEs, the panel believes that it is a best practice example that should be emulated by other members of the Evaluation Cooperation Group. The boards of MDBs should require independent confirmation that management has developed suitable M&E systems and uses the resulting information in their decision making.

The panel confirms the BROE's main findings that IFC has a sound M&E system for both projects and advisory services, the best for private sector operations among the MDBs. The system that has been set up by IFC management for monitoring and self-evaluation of its activities, which MIGA management is gradually trying to mirror, is impressive. The Development Outcome Tracking System, which measures development effectiveness, is now woven into the fabric of IFC, as demonstrated by the quality of its outputs and the increased use of the M&E findings in the preparation of new projects and advisory services, and in formulating strategies. The panel notes that all MDBs are struggling with evaluating the outcomes and impacts of advisory services. Given the cost implications, at best a sample of advisory services can be assessed at this level.

Convincing evidence is provided in the report to demonstrate that IFC and MIGA are improving their M&E systems. The BROE makes a compelling case that the information generated by a good M&E system can be used to support decision making in a manner that helps identify and correct problems, promotes leaning, and leads to achieving better development results.

The panel's positive view of the IFC M&E system is based on its design as a project company/client-centered system, despite some problems of relevance, timeliness, and data credibility that are documented in the report. IFC's M&E system generated evidence-based decision making and learning about risk and financial returns and social and environmental impacts. With few exceptions, the raw data in the M&E system are generated by IFC staff or by project companies, rather than from independent sources. This approach fits well with the perspective of a financier who wants to know whether a project is profitable and whether it meets defined environmental and social standards. Questions have been rightly asked in the BROE about the quality of the information that is provided by the project companies to the IFC and about the application of the verification mechanisms to secure data integrity. When dealing with the private sector and conducting self-evaluation, independent scrutiny of projects in the field is essential, as deficiencies in the project due diligence and structuring can often be better spotted during field visits.

To make investment decisions depend more on key development goals, IFC started its IFC Development Goals (IDG) system. It developed reach indicators to measure the wider impact of IFC investment and advisory projects. The report recognizes the associated challenges and warns that one needs to use the reach indicators in a balanced way. The M&E system does not focus on impacts on the final beneficiaries or generate and capture sufficient information about development-related impacts from primary sources. Meaningfully assessing the impact of a project on beneficiaries requires on-site data gathering. The stakeholder framework in figure A.1 is sound and provides an excellent foundation for assessing development impact. It identifies a broad range of stakeholders beyond the project company—neighborhood/environment, government/taxpayers, customers, producers of complimentary goods, competitors, suppliers, and employees. Although some of these groups are covered in the environment and social reports required by IFC, the BROE notes gaps and weaknesses in the data not obtained from verifiable sources for reach indicators, private sector development indicators, additionality, and development impact indicators.

The lack of information in the M&E system collected directly from a broader range of stakeholders may result in some "good news" stories not being reported or in obscuring some areas where remedial action is necessary. IFC and MIGA would enhance the credibility of their M&E systems if they used available and emerging information and communications technologies to gather first-hand (and timely) information from stakeholders other than IFC staff and project companies. The panel is mindful of the costs associated with primary data collection and believes that initially a highly selective approach should be used, focusing on projects that are likely to be controversial or to impact the lives of large numbers of people. With the advances in information and communications technology and social media, and the presence in many countries of active civil societies and third-party companies/institutions that have undertaken surveys, the cost of collecting and analyzing such primary data is decreasing to manageable levels. Several official and private aid organizations are using such feedback systems in guiding their strategies and policies (see Center for Global Development: http://blogs.cgdev.org/globaldevelopment/2013/01/make-a-consumer-reports-for-aid.php).

The panel reviewed the BROE's recommendations and supports them. The managements of IFC and MIGA, with one minor exception, endorsed the recommendations and outlined the steps that would be taken to address them. Management agreed that "IFC should conduct selective tests and reviews to validate information provided by clients" but disagreed that "the external assurance provider's mandate should be expanded to include assessment of the credibility and attribution of data—particularly related to IDGs—appropriate verification, and whether IFC is effectively disclosing data limitations or biases." The panel believes that the steps proposed by IFC management in this area are sound.

Based on its deliberations, the panel highlights several points made in the report that it feels are particularly important from a strategic perspective:

- **The importance of learning:** All MDBs are trying to become learning organizations and incorporate learning from past experience in the design of future operations, advisory services, strategies, and policies. This is proving to be a significant challenge. Compared with other MDBs, IFC is doing relatively well in this area, although there is clearly room for improvement. Senior management and the Board must constantly reinforce the culture of learning lessons from IFC's previous investment projects and advisory services during the appraisal, design, structuring, and approval stages. In the panel's review, the removal of the lessons section from the Project Data Sheet concept is a serious threat to the IFC as a learning institution. Reports that go to the Board for approval should have a section on lessons learned and an explanation of how the major lessons were used. If lessons were embedded in the approval process in a natural way, management would not see gathering lessons as an administrative burden.

- **Strengthening the M&E system for financial intermediation, global trade facility, and corporate-level transactions:** The IFC M&E system has its roots in traditional project lending and investment. The financial intermediary sector accounts for more than 50 percent of IFC investments. This type of intervention requires extra efforts to secure mandate compliance. As highlighted in the BROE, the Development Outcome Tracking System is not used for the short-term finance projects in the financial intermediary sector, in particular for the global trade finance facility. Corporate-level transactions are another type of intervention that is not well covered by the M&E system. Going forward, the M&E system needs to be fine-tuned to reflect the changes in the nature of IFC's portfolio. IEG has some evaluations in its pipeline that may provide some evidence that can help in addressing these issues.

- **Strengthening the coverage of higher-order projects in the self-evaluation system:** Some of the most influential evaluations undertaken in other MDBs were evaluations of higher-level products like strategies and policies. Cluster/sector reviews of all the major sectors in which IFC is working are essential for generating lessons that feed directly into, and help inform, new strategies and policies. Indeed, IEG is mandated to evaluate policies and strategies before they are revised. The IFC M&E system should be strengthened and broadened from its traditional project roots to cover some higher-order products. Ideally, a self-evaluation of those products should precede IEG's independent evaluations. In this context the panel welcomes the report's recommendation that "IFC's regional, country, industry sector, and Advisory Services business line strategies and initiatives should contain an explicit results matrix to assess strategic objectives, with relevant indicators to track progress and evaluate in a systematic manner, preferable embedded in periodic strategy updates." While IFC's M&E system is strong at the project level, the suggestion to include results-based matrices in other documents and to track the indicators would help IFC take the next step to broaden and strengthen the coverage of its M&E systems for these other products.

- **Assessing the quality of IFC's work for Advisory Services:** The report presents strong evidence that IFC's work quality, during both the preparation and supervisory phases, affects the results achieved by IFC-financed projects. In the panel's opinion, that analysis underlines the importance of the recommendation that "in the current process of revising [Project Completion Report] guidelines, IFC should include an assessment of IFC work quality in Advisory Services self-evaluations."

- **The importance of IFC's role and additionality:** The report rightly notes the distinction between development impact and IFC's role or additionality. Appendix A calls for an assessment of IFC's role and contribution. Because IFC should not proceed with a project in the absence of a clearly defined role/additionality, role/additionality should be a self-standing criterion and not be averaged with other indicators. A clear definition of additionality is crucial because the definition of additionalitiy determines the choice/construction of the counterfactual needed to assess whether additionality has been delivered.

- **Need for sustained effort and senior management attention to bring MIGA's M&E system up to the desirable level:** The panel agrees with the report's conclusion that MIGA has made significant progress during the last three years in implementing a functional M&E system. MIGA is improving its self-evaluation system and has recently formulated its own development goals-oriented system. Although it supports the report's recommendations related to MIGA's M&E system, the panel notes that the system is a work in progress. Sustained work and senior management attention will be needed over a period of several years to bring MIGA's system up to the desired levels, and that is consistent with the needs of an insurance underwriter.

The panel highlights one methodological/presentational issue that needs to be addressed during the preparation of future reports. Evidence from the surveys of various types of M&E users was discussed throughout the report. However, the response rates were low, ranging between 13 percent and 34 percent, and there were a limited number of responses in some categories. The panel estimated that, at the 95 percent confidence level, the sample error would be in the 5 percent to 10 percent range, depending on the response rate and distribution of responses, for the Investment and Advisory Services staff—more than 100 replies were received for each. However, for the MIGA staff involved in self-evaluation and the environmental and social staff, for which 13 and 20 responses, respectively, were received, the sample error could range between 11 percent and 22 percent.

Despite the fact that Appendix C states that the evaluation team undertook some consistency analysis of the survey results, the panel believes that good practice requires that readers be made explicitly aware of the level of statistical uncertainty associated with the survey results by disclosing it in the Limitations section. In the text IEG should suitably caveat the use of these data. For example, statements like "70 percent of staff members found…" are only appropriate if clear statistical evidence is presented that the survey respondents are representative of the survey population. The 20/30 percent of the staff members who responded to the survey had a motivation to do so. The nonresponding 70/80 percent did not share this motivation. The two groups may differ, which should be noted in the footnotes wherever the staff survey results are cited. Although the panel supports undertaking surveys of M&E users, IEG in collaboration with management must find ways to improve the response rates for its surveys.

Wilhelm Löwenstein
Managing Director, Institute of Development Research and Development Policy,
Ruhr University Bochum

Bruce Murray
Former Director General, Operations Evaluation Department, Asian Development
Bank

Fredrik Korfker
Former Chief Evaluator, Evaluation Department, European Bank for
Reconstruction and Development

Guy Pfeffermann
Founder and CEO, Global Business Network, and Former Chief Economist,
International Finance Corporation

Chapter 1

Context and Evaluation Framework

Chapter Highlights

- The private sector is essential to solving a wide range of development issues.
- The key function of monitoring and evaluation is to provide timely, credible, and reliable information to track progress on outcomes, assess performance, and generate knowledge of what works, what does not, and why.
- With the growing role of the private sector in development, the operations of IFC and MIGA have become more prominent in Bank Group activities and the institutions have upgraded their monitoring and evaluation systems apace with new responsibilities and emerging priorities.
- IFC has continuously strengthened monitoring and evaluation over the past 15 years; MIGA is implementing a self-evaluation system.

The prevailing development paradigm has shifted toward private investment, and the private sector has become an essential element of solutions to a broad range of development issues such as employment, education, health, food security, and social inclusion. The roles of the International Finance Corporation (IFC) and the Multilateral Investment Guarantee Agency (MIGA) have grown apace within the World Bank Group. Ten years ago they represented, respectively, 15 percent and 6 percent of the dollar volume of the Bank Group's financing activities; by 2012 IFC's share had risen to 29 percent and MIGA had kept its share at the same level.

There is great potential for the private sector to solve development problems and much to be learned about how to most effectively facilitate, mobilize, and utilize its contribution. For example, participants in the Fourth High-Level Forum on Aid Effectiveness in Busan, Republic of Korea, noted that effective aid involves participants beyond country governments, including civil society and the private sector. Effective monitoring and evaluating (M&E) systems are essential to learning and accountability on the best ways of catalyzing the private sector for development. They can provide timely, credible, and reliable information to track progress on outcomes, assess performance, and generate knowledge of what works, what does not, and why in efforts to promote private sector development. They also document results and accomplishments—by agency, department, or unit—relative to the resources that were allocated.

A results framework is an explicit articulation of the different levels, or chains, of results expected from a particular intervention—project, program, or development strategy (IEG 2012, p. 7). M&E can be a powerful tool that steers actions to results. The M&E[1] system comprises the process, methods, and tools for collecting data, tracking progress on outcomes and assessing performance and results. It has three main components: data collection, data quality control, and data analysis. The purpose of the system is to generate information to guide strategic planning, improve effectiveness and operational quality, and enhance accountability and learning. The value of a well-functioning M&E system has become apparent to development agencies, clients, and other stakeholders.

The two main organizational modes of evaluation are self-evaluation and independent evaluation. Both serve the purpose of learning and accountability and exist for different focus and emphasis. Self-evaluation is often embedded within the business processes. In contrast, independent evaluation is conducted with certain distance from management and may provide different insights because it avoids conflict of interest in rendering an objective and impartial assessment. IFC and MIGA each use both forms, with the Independent Evaluation Group (IEG) serving the role of independent evaluator. For IFC and MIGA, IEG conducts independent validations of projects' self-evaluations as well as independent evaluation of projects. IEG also evaluates sector, thematic, and corporate activities for both IFC and MIGA.

There has been a rapid evolution in IFC and MIGA M&E systems. Table 1.1 traces the expansion of instruments, activities, and systems since 1995. This evolution has occurred as the organizations adapted to changing and growing demands for their services from clients, donors, and development partners.

Table 1.1	Evolution of Private Sector Monitoring and Evaluation, 1995–2012		
	IFC		MIGA
	Investment and Corporate	Advisory Services	
1995–99	IFC had evaluation unit within Economics Department. 1996: Independent evaluation function, investment project evaluation 1998: Project self-evaluation pilot 1999: Enhancing coverage of self-evaluation (XPSR)		1996: First internal evaluations of MIGA projects
2000–04	2004: Management Action Tracking System		2002: Independent Evaluation function, project evaluation 2003: Management Action Tracking System 2004: Economic and Policy Group, Environmental and Social unit Business model emphasizing development role
2005	• Development Effectiveness Unit, Development Outcome Tracking System (DOTS) • IEG E&S Review reports attached to EvNotes		• Guidelines for assessing projects development impacts • Internal monitoring system (discontinued in 2007)
2006	• New sustainability policy, performance standard for Environmental and Social areas • New disclosure policy	Advisory Services results measurement pilot	• New guarantees procedures • Small Investment Program

(Table continues on the following page.)

Table 1.1	Evolution of Private Sector Monitoring and Evaluation, 1995–2012 (cont.)		
	IFC		
	Investment and Corporate	Advisory Services	MIGA
2007	• Development results re-porting in annual report, with external assurance review, Additionality Primer		MIGA's technical assistance integrated into Foreign Investment Advisory Services Policy on Social and Environmental Sustainability
2008		• Vice Presidency for Advisory Services; • Advisory Services Project Completion Report	
2009		Advisory Services branding in line with IFC	• Financial and operations Key Performance Indicators
2010	• DOTS 2 (new version of DOTS) • Additionality tracking • IDG pilot • Development Impact Department		• Self-evaluation pilot; • MIGA convention change (coverage of stand-alone debt, simplification of application, coverage of existing assets)
2011		• Advisory Services Operations Portal	Revised Underwriting Guideline; Environmental and Social Monitoring Strategy, Development Effectiveness Indicator System
2012	• IDG 2 and 3 go "live" • IFC's Environmental and Social Review Reports attached to XPSRs		

Sources: IFC and MIGA.
Note: IDG = IFC Development Goals; XPSR = Expanded Project Supervision Report.

In 1995 IFC's M&E was limited to selected number of projects for learning purposes. When the independent evaluation function was established in 1996, it expanded the scope of evaluation for a randomly selected representative sample of investment projects. A standardized evaluation framework was also introduced, which covered IFC investments to include development outcomes (that explicitly includes environmental and social reviews), the quality of IFC's work, and IFC's role and contribution to the project. IFC subsequently incorporated measuring development outcome into its Development Outcome Tracking System (DOTS), which has been applied to all investment operations since 2005; DOTS is tracking results against expected outcomes. In 2007, IFC adopted a "double bottom line," reporting DOTS-captured development results alongside its financial statements in its annual report. As its Advisory Services work increased, it developed systems for managing, monitoring, and evaluating those operations, which are embedded within its new information system platform, Advisory Services Operations Portal (ASOP). IEG evaluation of Environmental and Social Effects attached a separate

Environmental and Social (E&S) Review report to its Evaluative Notes in 2005; IFC followed suit in 2011 by attaching an E&S Review Report to Expanded Project Supervision Reports (XPSRs). It piloted IFC Development Goals (IDGs) in 2010 and is expanding them through IFC this year. In 2010 it established a Development Impact Department (CDI), encompassing both Investment and Advisory Services operations.

Since 1996, IFC has evolved from a state where it had no systematic data on its development accomplishments to having a system that documents with more than 300 quantitative indicators the development expectations and results to cover each project in its portfolio. It aggregates 15 standard indicators by department, region, sector, and the Corporation as a whole, and it discloses these data to the public.

MIGA enhanced its M&E efforts more recently, and its systems are not as extensive. Yet the nature of its business—political risk insurance as the only product and instrument with more remote relationship to the project enterprise than IFC—inherently limits the scope and depth of its M&E. It established an independent evaluation function in 2002, piloted self-evaluation in 2001, began tracking key performance indicators in 2009, and adopted a Development Effectiveness Indicator System (DEIS) in 2011.

IFC and MIGA managements also receive feedback from IEG on how they are implementing the IEG recommendations. These recommendations and subsequent follow-up has been tracked in the Management Action Record, which is jointly operated by Bank Group managements and IEG. This follow-up and reporting serve both accountability and learning functions. Through the Management Action Record, IEG and management monitor the degree to which the recommendations are implemented. Box 1.1 summarizes IEG recommendations from past reviews of M&E systems and management actions.

The purpose of this *Biennial Report on Operations Evaluation* is to provide an assessment of IFC's and MIGA's systems and inform the results agenda at IFC and MIGA. This evaluation updates the previous report in 2008 for IFC and expands its coverage to MIGA. It emphasizes the systems for gathering, analyzing, and using information as well as providing feedback that can strengthen the results focus in private sector operations. It takes stock of the results frameworks for development outcomes in IFC and MIGA determines whether they (1) provide reliable, timely, and useful monitoring information and self-evaluation evidence; (2) support evidence-based decision making and learning; and (3) result in improvements in the performance and results from IFC's or MIGA's activities.

M&E Systems for Development Results in IFC and MIGA

Table 1.2 summarizes the elements of IFC and MIGA M&E systems that span diverse activities from projects to corporate strategies. The foundations of these systems are self-evaluations that measure and assess project, program, and institutional performance at the project and strategic levels. At the early stage of project appraisal and screening, M&E activities include the designing of an

BROE 2008 Recommendations and Management Actions Records

The previous BROE (IEG 2008a) contained three recommendations to IFC management:

1. Enhance measurement of impact and additionality at the country level.
2. Achieve better coverage of IFC's portfolio in reporting on results.
3. Improve the quality of data in M&E.

These recommendations were retired from the Management Action Record during the last three years:

1. Enhance measurement of impact and additionality at the country level.
   Management viewed this recommendation as implemented in 2011, when IFC launched DOTS 2, which tracks IFC additionality in addition to development impact (IEG 2011, vol. 2, p. 141).

2. Achieve better coverage of IFC's portfolio in reporting on results.
   Management reported in 2012 that IFC reported more than 80 percent coverage for all 13 mandatory reach indicators for its active portfolio (IEG 2013, vol. 2, p. 157).

3. Strengthen oversight of M&E quality with proper record keeping functions.
   In 2010, management responded that this recommendation was implemented and retired it from tracking. The responses stated that the introduction of DOTS 2 would capture numerical data that allow for better aggregation. A data collection manual was finalized and training was offered to 1,406 participants in FY09 (IEG 2011, Vol. 2, p. 136).

IEG Recommendations to MIGA Management on Results Measurement

- IEG made various recommendations with regard to MIGA's results measurement in past evaluations. The following recommendations were retired in the last Management Action Record update.

- MIGA should consistency apply the ex ante development impact analysis for underwriting guarantees, including providing more focused training and incentives, to ensure the projects it supports are sound and have positive and sustainable development impact (IEG 2004).

- MIGA should strengthen its quality assurance especially before the project decision documents are finalized to ascertain that the analysis of project impacts is consistent with MIGA requirements and guidelines; are well documented; and are adequately reflected in the decision documents (IEG 2007).

- MIGA should carry out, on a pilot basis, a quality at entry self-assessment of a sample of new guarantees underwritten in FY07 to enhance institutional learning (IEG 2007).

- MIGA should adopt practical tools to guide the underwriting teams—such as sector-specific checklist and templates—in implementing its requirements and guidelines for development impact analysis (IEG 2007).

- Make significant progress in implementing initiatives related to development impact assessment and monitoring, recommended in previous evaluations of the Agency by IEG, including the development of self-evaluation (IEG 2008b).

- MIGA should strengthen and formalize its systems and standards for underwriting and introduce a robust quality assurance system for its operations as key elements of enhancing its overall institutional effectiveness (IEG 2009).

The following recommendations are still active, and progress has been reported in IEG's last MAR update (IEG 2013):

- Apply lessons from (self-) evaluation to future guarantee projects (IEG 2010b).
- Strengthen safeguards monitoring, evaluation, and completion reporting (IEG 2010a).

Source: IEG.

Table 1.2		Self-Monitoring and Evaluation Systems of IFC and MIGA		
		IFC		MIGA
		Investment	Advisory	
Project level	Monitoring	Development Outcome Tracking System E&S monitoring	Project Supervision Reports	Development Effectiveness Indicator System E&S monitoring program
	Self-evaluation	Expanded Project Supervision Reports with E&S Reviews Thematic and product assessment (some conducted by external parties/ consultants)	Project Completion Reports Thematic and product assessment (some by external parties/consultants)	Project Evaluation Reports
Program/sector/ country level	Monitoring	Department scorecards; country assessment	Advisory Services business line product-level monitoring/scorecards	
	Self-evaluation	Country Assistance Strategy Completion Reports		None
Corporate level	Monitoring	IFC Development Goals Scorecards		Development Effectiveness Indicator System
	Self-evaluation	Corporate reviews		Periodic review

Source: IEG.
Note: E&S = environmental and social.

ex ante results framework, specifying indicators, gathering baseline data, and setting targets. As projects are implemented, M&E facilitates data collection and tracking of performance.

Each component of an M&E system is organized by hierarchy, from project-level M&E to aggregated performance monitoring by country, region, and sector. M&E is intended to generate information and learning that feeds into higher-level strategies and ongoing operations, steers institutions, and provides incentives for positive outcomes.

IFC and MIGA's results framework are built from project data. IFC has separate frameworks for its two main business lines: Investment Services and Advisory Services. IFC and MIGA work with private businesses and public agencies to reach their development goals of economic growth and poverty reduction. Both organizations' systems are designed to strengthen the results focus and integrate them into the organizations' strategies for learning, accountability, and decision making.

IFC M&E Systems Overview

M&E for Investment Operations. IFC's investments comprise loans, equity investment, or guarantees to private enterprises[2] in developing countries. In addition to the monitoring system for managing financial risks and for various compliances such as environmental and social requirements and insurance coverage, IFC has developed distinctive results measurement frameworks for projects development outcome—widely accepted among private sector-oriented development finance institutions—that assess the results of the activities it finances, taking into account the impacts on all affected stakeholders. Findings are summarized in a performance matrix that includes market-based indicators, E&S standards, and project objectives (see Appendix A.1). These monitoring systems gather information until the IFC's financial exposure to the company ends.

Project monitoring focuses on measuring development results by gathering and processing information on indicators through DOTS. At the outset of a project, staff agree on specific, standardized, and measurable indicators, including baseline and targets. Performance is periodically tracked to provide feedback for operations work. At the strategic level, monitoring systems aggregate performance information by country, region, and client group. The results feed into IFC's strategies and ongoing operations.

Project evaluation was conducted through the annual XPSR program, which is the self-evaluation of IFC's investment projects. IDGs have been piloted as corporate-level development targets that capture the contributions from IFC's investment, advisory services as well as activities by its subsidiary Asset Management Company[3] that would help shape strategy and influence decision making. IFC started to implement IDG 2 and 3 in FY13. Once operational, the IDGs are expected to help implement the strategy and assess progress in achieving its double bottom line, development results and financial success.

M&E for Advisory Services. Through its Advisory Services operations, IFC provides advice, problem solving, and training to companies, industries, financial institutions, and governments. The framework for understanding the development impact of advisory services operations is based on the program logic model that links outcomes with project activities (see Appendix A.2).

Program Evaluation. IFC's program evaluations comprise donor-funded facility reviews, and thematic/product/program assessments of its operations. In addition, IFC staff or outside parties periodically evaluate projects and programs. At the strategic level, IFC has increased self-evaluation of Country Assistance Strategy Completion Reports (CASCRs), which are also reviewed by IEG.

MIGA M&E OVERVIEW

MIGA provides insurance against noncommercial risks for private investors and lenders in developing countries as well as public entities operating on a commercial basis; it also mediates investment disputes to support foreign direct investment. It covers the risk of expropriation, transfer restrictions, breach of contract, war and civil disturbance, and failure to meet sovereign financial obligations. As an insurer MIGA does not typically have inputs into project design or financial structuring. According to the latest underwriting guideline, the framework for assessing the results is similar to the one for IFC's investment, using the same stakeholder framework and benchmarks.

MIGA's current monitoring system is limited because of its business model—that of an insurance provider, it has more limited relationship with its clients. In FY11, MIGA introduced DEIS, which gathers standardized indicators for each project. It compiles baseline data at the beginning of projects and updates it three years after approval of guarantees.

MIGA's evaluation system has evolved over the past decade. IEG has independently evaluated MIGA guarantee projects since 2003, but MIGA did not have a self-evaluation system before 2010. MIGA's management committed to producing self-evaluations systematically and IEG continues to evaluate a sample of guarantee projects annually, on top of validation of self-evaluations.

At the corporate level, MIGA provides a periodic review of its activities and results as mandated in its Convention. It introduced five key performance indicators that measure its performance and productivity: (1) volume of guarantees issues, (2) the number of projects supported, (3) guarantees in IDA (International Development Association) countries, (4) MIGA's return on operating capital, and (5) ratio of administrative expenses/net premium income.

Normative Standard for Assessing Monitoring and Evaluation Systems and Evaluation Framework

This evaluation uses a results-based model of M&E. Traditional M&E is implementation oriented, looking at inputs and milestones. Results-based M&E tracks outputs, achievements, and results to assess achievements and reflect findings in ongoing activities. An effective system should provide credible, reliable evidence about performance. It should collect reliable data, store it an accessible database, control data quality, and provide for analysis and interpretation (Goergens and Kusek 2010). Results-based M&E has six characteristics:

- Baseline data that show the pre-intervention status
- Indicators for outcomes and results
- Changes (and perceptions of changes) among stakeholders are evidence of results
- Data on outputs and their contributions to outcomes
- Systemic progress assessments
- Judgments on success and failure in achieving desired outcomes.

M&E systems can be applied to different levels of activity: project, program, sector, country, and institution. The indicators, data complexity, and uses of information may vary, but the system should be aligned among levels to permit linkages between policies, programs and projects (Kusek and Rist 2004; Morra and Rist 2009). There are five characteristics of a good M&E system:

- Usefulness—Helps to clarify goals and objectives and supporting selection of good strategies, projects, or approaches.

- Feedback—Provides timely and reliable knowledge of what works, what doesn't, and why.

- Transparency and accountability—Gives the data necessary to determine how well the institution and its operational units are performing.

- Effectiveness—The extent to which the system contributes to better outcomes.

- Efficiency—Costs relative to effectiveness.

Figure 1.1 illustrates the conceptual framework linking activities to results of M&E systems. The foundations of an M&E system are its data and the components related to collecting and verifying data. The reliability of the system depends on the quality and quantity of the data it has. Indicators are the data that illustrate progress toward achievement of results when they are compared against the baseline and target. In the end, the data are only valuable if they provide credible and reliable information about performance.

This evaluation has three sets of evaluative questions related to the conceptual framework in figure 1.1. The first set focuses on credibility of data and the systems for gathering data, ensuring data quality, and analyzing data. The second set evaluates the utility of the information for tracking progress and improving decision making. The last set of questions pertains to whether M&E has improved the quality of strategies, projects, and development outcomes.

The overarching evaluation question is: Are the M&E systems of IFC and MIGA equipped to inform the organizations on their performance and results? The underlying specific evaluation questions are as follows:

1. What are the mechanisms for ensuring that M&E systems generate credible, timely, and relevant information?

   1.1. What are the processes, methods, and tools for gathering data, and how effective are they in terms of producing information?

Figure 1.1	Results Chain of M&E

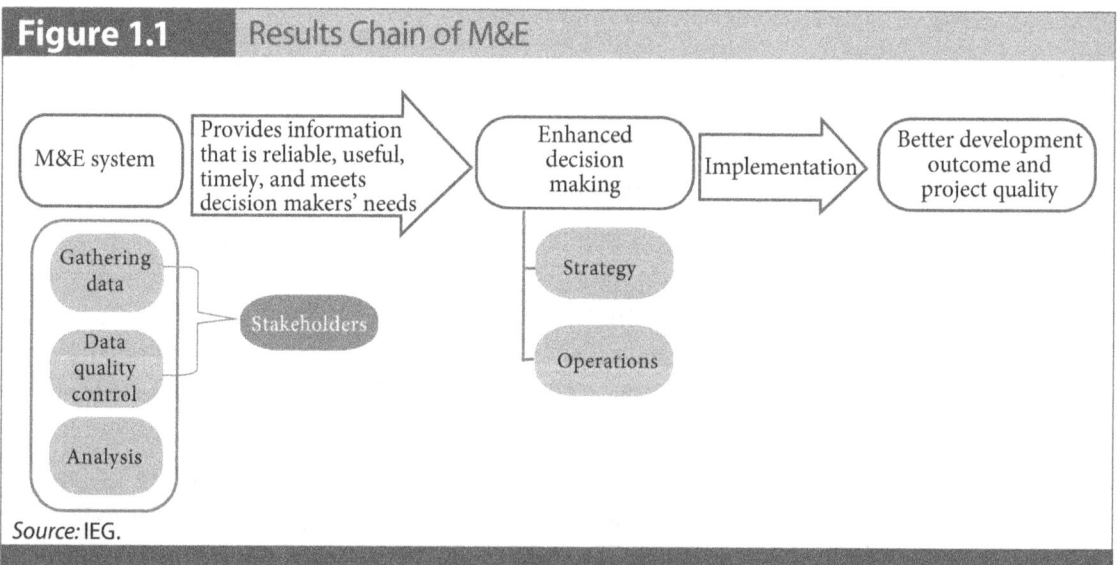

Source: IEG.

1.2. What are the processes, methods, and tools for quality control of collected data, and how effective and efficient are they in terms of ensuring quality?

1.3. What are the processes, methods, and tools for data analysis, and how effective are they in producing information?

2. To what extent does M&E information support evidence-based decision making and learning?

2.1. To what extent is monitoring information used to make adjustments during project and strategy implementation?

2.2. To what extent is monitoring information used for in-depth assessment of issues?

2.3. To what extent is information from M&E used to learn lessons from project performance?

3. What has been the impact of the M&E outputs and use on project quality and development outcomes?

3.1. To the extent that M&E outputs have been used, has the result been better development outcomes and project quality?

3.2. To the extent that impacts on development outcomes and project quality can be ascertained, are these impacts commensurate with costs?

Methodology

IEG used multiple instruments in this evaluation: desk reviews of policies and procedures, a sample of project-level M&E data, various internal databases, internal memos and strategic documents, and interviews and surveys of staff and management. These sources meet the evaluative inquiries targeted to particular business segments and M&E characteristics. Table 1.3 lays these out in more detail, relating the activities to sources.

IEG compares existing M&E policies, procedures, and practices with established standards such as the Good Practice Standards for private sector evaluation of the Evaluation Cooperation Group (ECG) for multilateral development banks (ECG 2011a). These cover project-level evaluation for IFC investment activities and MIGA guarantees, as well as factors associated with well-functioning M&E systems (Kusek and Rist 2004; Morra and Rist 2009; Goergens and Kusek 2010; IEG 2012).

Limitations

The evaluation is focused on the functioning and the quality of IFC and MIGA's systems for development results. It does not evaluate results; these are covered comprehensively in other evaluations (IEG 2013).[4] The report does not cover the World Bank's M&E systems.

Independent evaluation is important in the results frameworks of IFC and MIGA. However, IEG focuses on monitoring and self-evaluation in these institutions, and the role and contribution of IEG are outside the scope of this evaluation. IEG

Table 1.3	Methodologies to Evaluate IFC and MIGA's M&E Systems	
Evaluation activities	Focus	Sources
Analysis of IFC and MIGA policies and guidelines on M&E	System analysis (relevance, timeliness)	IFC and MIGA policies and guideline
Analysis of M&E data from IFC investment projects including E&S aspects	Quality of information[a]	DOTS and XPSR data for projects: XPSRs: All XPSRs validated by IEG between 1996 and 2011 (n = 920) XPSR sample: Random selected XPSR projects from 2008 to 2011 (n = 70) Random sample of projects committed between 2008 and 2011 (n = 90) out of population of 1,365
Analysis of M&E data from IFC advisory services projects	Quality of information[a]	M&E information for projects: PCRs validated by IEG between 2008 and 2010 (n = 280) PCR sample: Random sample of above projects (n = 71)
Analysis of M&E data for MIGA guarantee projects including E&S aspects	Quality of information[a]	PERs: 26 projects with PER (7 were self-evaluations with IEG validation, 19 were produced by IEG) between 2008 and 2011 Sample of projects after formal introduction of DEIS (n = 23) out of population of 50 underwritten in FY11.
Analysis of M&E database	Quality of information[a]	Catalogue of M&E reports commissioned by IFC
Analysis of department strategies	Use and influence of M&E information[b]	IFC department (regions, sector) business strategies that are prepared between 2010 and 2012 during the annual corporate strategy discussions
Meta analysis of IFC corporate strategies	Use and influence of M&E information[b]	IFC Road Map (with Corporate Scorecard) 2010–13
Interviews	Use and influence of M&E information[b]	Semistructured interviews to IFC and MIGA staff and managers (57)
Staff surveys	Use and influence of M&E information[b]	IFC investment staff (n = 118) IFC advisory services staff (n = 138) IFC economist, strategists, M&E staff, DOTS champions and Development Impact Department staff (n = 33) IFC environmental and social specialists (n = 20) MIGA staff involved in self-evaluation pilot (n = 13)
Analysis of Budget data	Efficiency of M&E	IFC database
Meta analysis of lessons archival systems	Use and influence of M&E information[b]	IFC's SmartLessons IEG's E-LRN
Meta analysis of ECG documents	Benchmark	Third Benchmarking Review of Evaluation Cooperation Group members evaluation practices for their private sector investment operations against their agreed good practice standards (ECG 2011b)
Case examples	Use and influence of M&E information[b]	IFC agribusiness projects (XPSRs and lessons)

Source: IEG.
Note: DEIS = Development Effectiveness Indicator System; DOTS = Development Outcome Tracking System; ECG = Evaluation Cooperation Group; M&E = monitoring and evaluation; PCR = Project Completion Report; PER = Project Evaluation Report; XPSR = Expanded Project Supervision Report.
a. Quality of information includes relevance, credibility, and timeliness of information.
b. Use and influence of M&E information includes relevance and timeliness of information.

recently completed a self-evaluation of its activities and the Board commissioned an independent assessment of IEG's activities.

This evaluation does not cover CASCRs. IFC has participated in the self-evaluation of Country Assistance Strategies since 2007, but its participation is selectively focused on private sector activities, which are a niche within the overall Bank Group Country Assistance Strategy. The strategy process and products are fully integrated with the World Bank, and IEG does not evaluate the limited IFC-related items within the CASCRs in this report.

Finally, external stakeholders such as clients, donors, and cofinanciers are important partners, and their contributions, perspectives, and uses of M&E information are important. However, this evaluation focuses on the IFC and MIGA's institutional arrangements for M&E.

Notes

1. Although M&E are complementary, each element performs a separate and distinct role in a results framework (Kusek and Rist 2004, p. 14). *Monitoring* translates objectives into performance indicators and sets targets. It routinely collects data to give information on where a policy, program, or project is relative to targets and outcomes. Information from a monitoring system reports progress on outcomes, and provides evidence for making adjustments during project implementation. *Evaluation* provides a more systematic assessment of planned, ongoing, or completed interventions. It provides insights into why intended results were achieved or not and on the causal relationships between interventions and results. Evaluation can therefore be more detailed and time consuming and cost more.

2. In some cases, IFC and MIGA support government-owned investment, if the entities are operating in a commercial basis. For instance, this might include power companies or telecommunications providers that operate like a commercial company, charging market rates.

3. Investment projects through the Asset Management Company are tracked by DOTS, as its investee clients are also IFC's investment clients.

4. The most recent *Results and Performance of the World Bank Group 2012* (IEG 2013) covers the performance of the World Bank Group operations, including IFC and MIGA, as well as the key new development of results framework of the World Bank, and tracking of Managements' action in responses to the past IEG recommendations.

References

ECG (Evaluation Cooperation Group). 2011a. *Good Practice Standards for Evaluation of Private Sector Operations,* rev. ed. http://www.ecgnet.org/gps/.

———. 2011b. *Third Benchmarking Review of ECG Members' Evaluation Practices for Their Private Sector Investment Operations against Their Agreed Good Practice Standards.* http://www.ecgnet.org.

Goergens, M., and J. Kusek. 2010. *Making Monitoring and Evaluation Systems Work.* Washington DC: World Bank.

IEG (Independent Evaluation Group). 2004. *Review of Development Effectiveness in MIGA.* Washington, DC: World Bank.

———. 2007. *IEG-MIGA Annual Report.* Washington, DC: World Bank.

———. 2008a. *Biennial Report on Operations Evaluation: IFC's Results Measurement for Better Results.* Washington, DC: World Bank.

———. 2008b. *IEG-MIGA Annual Report.* Washington, DC: World Bank.

———. 2009. *Independent Evaluation of MIGA's Development Effectiveness—2009.* Washington, DC: World Bank.

———. 2010a. *Safeguards and Sustainability Policies in a Changing World.* Washington, DC: World Bank.

———. 2010b. *Independent Evaluation of MIGA's Development Effectiveness—2010.* Washington, DC: World Bank.

———. 2011. *Results and Performance of the World Bank Group: IEG Annual Report 2011.* Washington, DC: World Bank.

———. 2012. *World Bank Group Impact Evaluations: Relevance and Effectiveness.* Washington, DC: World Bank.

———. 2013. *Results and Performance of the World Bank Group 2012.* Washington, DC: World Bank.

Kusek, J., and R. Rist. 2004. *Ten Steps to a Result-Based Monitoring and Evaluation System.* Washington DC: World Bank.

Morra, L., and R. Rist. 2009. *The Road to Results: Designing and Conducting Effective Development Evaluations.* Washington DC: World Bank.

Chapter 2

Monitoring and Evaluation in
IFC and MIGA

This chapter assesses IFC's and MIGA's systems for M&E with a focus on the process, methods, and tools for data gathering, quality control, and data analysis. These systems provide project-level information that can be aggregated to represent the development outcomes that the institutions have achieved.

This chapter is organized in line with evaluation question 1. There are three distinct M&E systems: for IFC Investment Services, IFC Advisory Services, and MIGA guarantees. These systems support activities and decision making at the project, program, and corporate levels. At each level, there are activities classified as monitoring and self-evaluation. The subsequent sections give a descriptive analysis and findings on the processes, methods, and instruments for data gathering, quality control and data analysis.

Monitoring and Evaluation for IFC Investment Operations

IFC has multiple systems to monitor its investments. The credit risk rating (CRR) system is used for monitoring financial risk. Each financial exposure is assessed quarterly to predict the possibility of asset impairment over the next two years. The system is linked to IFC's Capital, Pricing and Risk system for comprehensive financial risk management.

Supplementing the CRR, IFC has systems with its clients' financial information to value its equity investments and to monitors clients' insurance. IFC's E&S reviews track compliance with E&S requirements and provide Environmental and Social Risk Ratings for projects. CRRs are updated quarterly and Environmental and Social Risk Ratings are typically updated annually and after site visits. Until 2011, Project Supervision Reports (PSRs)[1] were prepared annually for investment projects, but IFC discontinued them to simplify its processes.

IFC is a strong player among PSD agencies in monitoring, evaluating, and disclosing its development results. Its M&E system compares favorably with those of other development banks. According to one study, the strength of IFC's DOTS approach is based on the level of detail it provides with respect to quantitative and qualitative development indicators that are relevant to different industries and sectors (Dalberg Global Development Advisors 2010, p. 26). IFC has also contracted external assurance by independent auditors for its development information[2] (Nathan Associates 2011, p. 40). IFC is also active in discussions of multilateral development banks' (MDBs') Common Performance Assessment System), which aims to develop and strengthen corporate results monitoring systems. Similarly, the United Kingdom's Department for International Development commended IFC for its "strong strategic and performance management with a leading results framework and effective use of evaluation" (DFID 2011, p. 90), and "IFC's results framework is recognized as a leading example among development finance institutions" (p. 185).

DOTS is used to systematically monitor development results of IFC's investments. DOTS follows the investment project cycle from screening and appraisal until closure. The system has three functions: (1) recording and tracking performance indicators, (2) assigning performance ratings, and (3) assessing "additionality" (that is, the special role IFC expects to play). DOTS includes all IFC investments and is updated annually.

"AT ENTRY" FOUNDATIONS FOR MONITORING

DOTS is based on the development results framework for IFC investments (see Appendix A.1), which follows IFC's ex post evaluation framework. The information system platform for DOTS was upgraded in 2008. One new feature was the complete coverage over a project's life cycle. DOTS data on a project or company flow directly into relevant project-cycle documents at each decision stage, from concept review to Board approval[3] and throughout supervision.

IFC conducts an E&S assessment for each project based on the 2006 Policy on Social and Environmental Sustainability (revised in 2012) and its Environmental and Social Review Procedure. These documents describe the roles and responsibilities of IFC and its client companies at appraisal and supervision. IFC receives from clients Annual Monitoring Reports and reviews them against E&S requirements, including IFC Performance Standards and Environmental, Health and Safety Guidelines to establish Environmental and Social Risk Rating, and to give feedback to clients. In addition, IFC's Environmental and Social Specialists visit projects with high E&S risks or information gaps. IFC records ratings for Performance Standard indicators at appraisal and monitoring in an online Environmental and Social Review Document (ESRD).

CHOOSING INDICATORS AND SETTING TRACKING PARAMETERS

Indicators are established at the early project review stage to appraise a project's impacts on each stakeholder group. There are two categories: standard departmental indicators and customized indicators. The former set was established for each industry and covers its particular development results. When a project is processed at the review stage, the relevant DOTS mandatory indicators are mapped automatically to the project by sector. However, there seems to be a trade-off between standardization and relevance of indicators in the specific project context. In the staff survey, 42 percent of staff handling appraisals said the mandatory indicators for DOTS are not sufficient to represent a project's development impacts.

IFC measures its reach by the number of people touched by its activities, and 15 of the standard indicators are reach indicators—which are presented as "Development Reach by IFC's Investment Clients" in the IFC annual report. They represent companies' outputs and outcomes, but not impacts. Reach data allow IFC to portray the direct footprint of the projects and companies it supports. In the 2008 Biennial Review of Operations Evaluation, IEG described coverage gaps in indicators: 41 percent of client companies and 62 percent of clients in Sub-Saharan Africa were not included in reach estimates. IFC has narrowed this gap, and in FY11 more than 80 percent of active clients were represented in the annual report. IFC also reports contextual information as footnotes in some reports (for example, the IFC annual report). These footnotes usually describe anomalies, such as very large contributors to a reach number, fluctuations from portfolio movements, or possible effects of IFC Advisory Services on a client.

The use of indicators in Board reports has increased. About 30 percent of the sampled projects approved between 2003 and 2006 (mostly before IFC introduced DOTS) and evaluated in 2008–11 cited a limited number of quantifiable indicators such as financial or economic rate of return. Other nonquantifiable indicators were referred to as indicators that will be tracked in the PSR.

In the sample of Board reports from 2008–11 commitments had better indicators and formats. The clearest format was a matrix, with indicators classified by performance area, and with columns for expected development impact, indicator name, baseline and target information, and data source. These indicators were transferred to DOTS for monitoring. However, 13 percent of the sample reports did not include three or more indicators in the Board report to DOTS. Often, nonstandard indicators were not transferred from Board documents to DOTS without records of droppages, although project teams are free to add custom indicators in DOTS.

Often projects seek private sector development (PSD), such as improved competition, demonstration effects of a business model, or sectoral transformations. However, there are several gaps in DOTS for tracking PSD. First, only a few indicators are used for PSD. Less than half (46 percent) of the projects in the XPSR sample (2008–11) used those indicators. Second, even though there are indicators for PSD, they only contain the indicators that are not relevant to the objectives at entry (for example, only indicators used were about corporate governance, although the stated objectives did not have such objectives). In the same sample, only 28 percent of projects had DOTS indicators that had direct relevance to the PSD expectations in the Board report.

For example, although the project objective states that investments in second or third entrants will enhance sectoral competition, or increased market participants and innovation by demonstration of commercial success, there were no indicators associated with these effects. Furthermore, many DOTS indicators (such as increased competition, adoption of best practice, or demonstration effects) were judged by answering "yes" or "no" without providing objective measures.

More recent approvals have greater relevance between objectives and indicators, but a gap remains. About 40 percent of the sample of recent projects (committed between 2008 and 2011) did have PSD indicators in DOTS that were relevant to expected outcomes. But the disconnects are still significant, because, according to DOTS rating guidelines, PSD is to be rated according to progress against the at-entry objectives.

ASSIGNING PERFORMANCE RATINGS DURING SUPERVISION

The next important function of DOTS is tracking ratings during supervision. Projects that are sufficiently mature (at least 12 months of operating results) are expected to be rated on their development dimensions. The ratings are assigned annually and subject to change as projects mature and more results emerge.

Projects are monitored by portfolio officers (normally different from those who appraised the project) who manage client relationships and E&S specialists who monitor the E&S components.[4] Once indicators have been rated against targets, ratings are assigned for four performance areas—financial, economic, environmental and social, and PSD—corresponding to the stakeholders in the stakeholder analysis. For economic performance, the indicators are benchmark-based figures such as economic return on invested capital, supplemented by other indicators. E&S is based on compliance with applicable standards. PSD dimensions are assessed by comparing results against the original objectives in the Board report. Ratings measure actual performance against the targets but are also based on judgments of other unquantifiable development outcomes. These four ratings are synthesized into a judgment of overall project success.

The third monitoring function is to collect data on additionality. Additionality refers to IFC's unique role and contribution to a project's success, which would not be available from commercial sources. In 2007, IFC distributed an "additionality primer" to help staff develop, assess, and communicate IFC's role and contribution more systematically and effectively. It established four categories of additionality: risk mitigation, knowledge and innovation, standard setting, and policy work. Like development outcome indicators, DOTS is designed to monitor aspects of additionality that appeared in the Board report, assign the additionality to one of the four categories, and estimate when it will be realized. The assessment addresses whether the expected additionality is achieved and it is reviewed annually.

Additionality tracking is new, as this was introduced in 2011 when IFC launched DOTS 2 as a part of system upgrade. IFC put efforts on backfilling the additionality information as well as recording achievement on yearly basis. So far, among IEG's review of 2008–11 commitments,[5] only five projects had no tracking information on additionality.

DATA GATHERING

The first source of data is the client: audited financial statements, other reports, and additional information requested by IFC. According to the staff survey conducted for this evaluation, client information is the dominant source. Eighty-two percent of survey respondents used client data in some form, even for nonfinancial information. Sixty-eight percent used audited financials and 65 percent use corporate annual reports. Use of other data sources has been limited. Thirty-eight percent of survey respondents used third-party data (including government statistics and/or international databases, excluding data from the client), and 36 percent referred to data within IFC.

IFC's portfolio has increasingly been concentrated in the financial sector. About half of the current portfolio is financial market, and during the past five years, there have been surges in guaranteeing short-term finance through trade finance programs such as the Global Trade Finance Facility. Increased "wholesaling" of IFC support through financial intermediaries is associated with more efficient delivery of IFC financing.

However, the wholesaling approach poses several challenges for tracking and assessing results. First, the short-term finance projects had not been covered by the DOTS results framework. The approval documents are streamlined and do not have specific discussions of expected outcomes at the transaction level or indicators for development results.

Second, measuring development results of financial projects at the sub-borrower level (or the level of end beneficiaries) is inherently difficult, and IFC has gaps in information. IFC has no direct relationship with, access to, or often even knowledge of the companies or microenterprises that are borrowing from the financial institutions. In practice, DOTS tracking for indicators such as number of small and medium-size enterprise (SME) borrowers is based on "proxy" figures from the financial institutions' portfolio: number of loans below a maximum, the total portfolio of the targeted business segment (such as housing, energy efficiency), and the credit quality of that portfolio (such as number of nonperforming loans).

IFC recently surveyed 34 banks in 25 countries and looked at 3,157 SME loans (based on the proxy) to determine whether the recipients are actually SMEs. It found that 63 percent of the credit files had sufficient information on employees, assets, and sales. Based on that, IFC mapped the micro, small, and medium-size enterprise (MSME) definition; 80 percent would have been defined as SMEs and 18 percent as microenterprises. Only 2 percent would not be classified as SMEs. However, there was considerable overlap among the micro, small, and medium categories.

Also, these indicators reveal little about the intermediary's record of extending credit to the most productive companies or the impacts. Although nonperforming loans of specific segments of financial intermediary clients are used as a proxy for the business performance of the sub-borrowers, the consideration of collaterals and other risk mitigations can hide the poor business performance of the financial institution clients. Often, IFC sets targets of extending loans to groups of previously unbanked microentrepreneurs, yet the extent to which borrowers had been previously unbanked cannot be confirmed because of a lack of data. Given that the client does not collect and report on whether new subborrowers had previously borrowed from the formal financial sector, it is not possible to assess reliably whether borrowers had been previously "unbanked." Assumption of new clients as fresh entrants to formal financial institutions needs to be questioned.

Third, IFC's funding relative to the intermediary's total assets is usually small. Money is fungible, so attributing subprojects to IFC's intervention is arbitrary. Moreover, these indicators do not indicate long-term access to financing after IFC's credit line ends—the bank may terminate the line of business when IFC exits, so an increased access to financing may be transitory.

Fourth, assessing E&S effects of financial intermediary projects is also challenging because of the often weak capacity of local financial intermediaries to ensure that subprojects meet IFC's requirements (usually Host Country Laws and Exclusion List, and for high-risk projects IFC's Performance Standards). Also the subproject clients do not have legal responsibility to IFC for their E&S effects.

Quality Control

Data supplied to IFC must to be validated for credibility and relevance before being incorporated into IFC's results measurement system. Quality control is partly structural: standard indicators are defined so they can be taken from standard documentation for any type of client. This would include audited financial reports, company annual reports, and other sources with built-in validation.

Data are timely when they are up to date and the information is available when it is needed. DOTS data are entered as they become available, or entries are updated at least annually and information is provided per the client's reporting cycle. DOTS is a central element to the supervision cycle, which begins after the first disbursement, when a project is passed to portfolio officers for supervision, and ends with project closure. During supervision, each project indicator is updated annually and IFC diligently follows clients' audited financial statements. There are similar reporting requirements for annual E&S monitoring. The information is tied to respective risk rating systems (CRR and Environmental and Social Risk Ratings), so follow-up actions are triggered if there are discrepancies.

In the data manual for DOTS, CDI cites the four data quality considerations—accountability, consistency with previous years' data, consistency in definitions, and focus on the target of IFC investment. For new business, the department emphasizes consistency between DOTS and Board report data. This department oversees the annual DOTS quality control cycle. The schedules start in January by naming clients to be included in the six-year rolling cycle for the annual report. Data collection and entry are coordinated during February to April in operational departments for the reach data. Data completion and quality review take place between March and May. Data analysis and reporting are completed by the end of fiscal year (June 30). Based on IEG's review of a sample of projects, all active projects (except trade finance which does not use DOTS) had entries for the last fiscal year.

The annual quality control review[6] covers ratings, rationales, and flags for selected indicators (see table 2.1). Quality control has two main components. The first is a systematic but focused mechanism that tracks big contributions and big variations.[7] The second occurs after information has been filed[8] and is focused on ratings and figures for the annual report. Indicators that are not mandatory and are not in the annual report are not monitored by the process and fall under the portfolio review. Data are deemed reliable after the annual quality control process.

CDI does not contact clients but relies on IFC's supervisory staff. There is no third-party validation of the data from project companies; data are mainly checked against existing projects.

As part of the quality control process, CDI checks with investment staff on reach data from the biggest contributors. Some indicators are dominated by a small group of clients; one company accounts for 91 percent of gas distribution and eight firms for 68 percent of IFC's patients reached. The two most frequent sources of information are company reporting materials (some are from audited financial statements) and verifications from company personnel. In some cases, CDI officers

Table 2.1	Flags Used in DOTS Quality Control	
Type of Flag	Meaning	Action required
Old not rated	Companies that are likely to require a rating given the maturity of their first active project. In general, any project approved more than three years ago should be rated.	Rate or justify too-early-to-tell ratings (for example, "Project still under construction").
Young but rated	Companies with project(s) approved less than two years ago, but that already have performance ratings.	Ensure that the ratings are justified (for example, expansion of existing operation, short implementation period with early results).
ODO inconsistency	Three or more performance areas rated but not ODO.	Rate ODO.
DOTS internal mismatch	Apparent discrepancy between ODO and four performance areas.	Revise ratings to be consistent, or ensure clear rationale is provided to explain the apparent discrepancy.
Indicator inconsistency	ODO rated but three or more performance areas are not.	Rate the performance areas or re-evaluate ODO rating.
Financial impact	Discrepancy between financial performance rating and CRR.	Justify the discrepancy or re-evaluate the performance area rating.
E&S impact	Discrepancy between E&S performance rating and ESRR.	Justify the discrepancy or re-evaluate the performance area rating.

Source: IFC.
Note: CRR = credit risk rating; DOTS = Development Outcome Tracking System; E&S = environmental and social; ESRR = Environmental and Social Risk Rating; ODO = overall development outcome.

ask investment officers about the data sources of figures in the DOTS, as well as for explanations of large decreases in new employment figures. At the end of FY12, CDI reviewed reach data from 68 companies that contributed large shares to reach indicators.

For the FY12 review, CDI officers requested further clarification of numbers; there were unfulfilled data requests for six companies as of July 2012. Some reach data were cross-checked with public data. Infrastructure indicators (phone connections, power generation/distribution, and water and gas distribution) and transport indicators used third-party data, most frequently government websites. For example, for "airline passengers," three of the four clients mentioned government taxes paid to validate the number of passengers.

In contrast, some indicators were based on assessment. For example, 25 percent of total annual "number of farmers reached" was derived from two client companies. These numbers were based on estimates by company or investment staff. For one project, the client company made the estimate, as it makes purchases without direct contact with farmers who work with the suppliers and is unable to obtain actual numbers from the farmers. Therefore, the company came up with an estimate with the managers of its operating factories.

Similarly, the number of MSMEs reached is also estimated, but reach data are neither mandated nor collected by the client companies (totaling 63 percent of portfolio share). Estimates are based on total volume of MSME trade divided by average volume traded by one MSME. As the indicators are part of the corporate goal in the proposed IDG, it may be worthwhile for IFC to make extra efforts to validate figures for some large contributors by testing the assumptions and fine-tuning the estimation methodology.

A data quality review template is used, and communications (such as emails from clients) are kept in the project record. The feedback and discussion on data consistency and data sources are not entered in DOTS, and DOTS does not have a trace of data reviews. Ratings and reach data for publication (as well as external assurance) are a separate "proof" database, not in DOTS. The system does not have fields to indicate how data are to be gathered or the name of a company contact. This is a risk to continuity and data integrity in the face of frequent staff turnover in IFC and its clients.

IFC contracts for an external quality assurance review on select development information in its annual report, including quantitative indicators and qualitative statements. This started when IFC first reported DOTS information in its 2007 annual report.[9] The review aims to provide assurance that indicators complied with the relevant standards[10] and that the report meets IFC's policy on Disclosure of Information (IFC 2012, p. 103).

Quality assurance is limited to specific statements in the annual report (box 2.1). The quantitative review draws on consolidated corporate-level data and chooses its sample as a combination of extremes (flagged risk areas) and a sample of the middle. Of the five areas where the reporting criteria are assessed, only ex post

The scope of external assurance of nonfinancial information in the IFC annual report is based on the reporting criteria, policies, and principles for relevance, completeness, neutrality, clarity, and reliability. This involves (1) identification and review of key statements in the annual report, (2) interviews to assess the application of reporting criteria or to substantiate statements, (3) analytical verification (on a test basis) of the calculations and consolidation of indicators, and (4) documentation review. The review of the 2011 annual report notes progress in strengthening internal controls for development effectiveness of advisory services and carbon footprint but recommends improvements of reporting tools and internal controls for indicators relating to investments in renewable energy and energy efficiency.

Assurance coverage for the 2012 annual report has a similar scope. The reporting criteria are reviewed for advisory services, investment services, energy efficiency and renewable energy, MSMEs, and carbon footprint. The assurance group visited the Istanbul field office as part of its review of Investment and Advisory Services, although this was an informal pilot.

Source: IEG.

MSME data are assured; that is, only 1 of 15 measures of Development Reach by IFC Investment Clients. Moreover, like CDI's quality control, the assurance group's review does not include contacting clients, visiting projects, or communicating with field-based staff. Assurance is limited to desk reviews and does not involve verifying data from clients.

In short, data quality control timing has been driven by the external reporting cycle and the annual report. The checks are mainly desk based, and there is no data verification at the source. Some direct data verification for very specific areas (critical information that feeds into IDG and is largely calculated based on certain assumptions, instead of audited numbers or verifiable through public records) would enhance the credibility and reliability of the data supplied by the companies and staff.

Self-Evaluation of IFC Investments

XPSRs are the primary instrument of self-evaluation for investments. Investment staff prepare XPSRs for a random, representative sample of mature projects selected by IEG. The XPSR is a detailed, once-in-a-lifetime evaluation. It involves recalculation of financial and economic models and independent judgment of a project's likely effects. For the XPSR, the E&S specialist evaluates the project's E&S effects based on E&S performance indicators at the time of evaluation and E&S impacts, which include projects wider impacts in the region and sector and overall change of E&S performance from appraisal to evaluation. IEG independently reviews each project's performance, based on project documents and the XPSR with selective field validation. The XPSR assesses an operation's success with four areas that reflect financial, economic, and E&S performance and the contribution to PSD. It also reflects assessments on the quality of IFC's work and a project's contribution to IFC's profits. The completed XPSRs are independently validated by IEG, which prepares an Evaluative Note on each.

On-time completion of XPSRs has been a problem. There is "bunching" of XPSRs: nearly half are submitted during November and December every year. The 2010 program was the first that IFC did not complete before the end of the program year.

QUALITY OF XPSRs

Although IEG provides instructions and guidance on XPSR preparation to the XPSR teams, the team and its managers are responsible for contents, analysis, and judgment in the XPSR. IEG evaluates the quality of XPSRs and rates some as "good practice" as a preliminary screening for selection of IEG awards to XPSR teams for "the best" XPSR of the year. There is no fixed number to be judged as good practice each year, and the criteria are scope, responsiveness, and objectivity in assigning ratings; candidness of presenting the findings; internal consistency; and quality of lessons in the XPSR. By this standard, XPSR quality rose steadily through 2007 but has dropped in the past few years (figure 2.1). In 2007, 30 XPSRs met the "good practice" criteria—more than half the XPSRs. However, the number fell to 19 (of 77 XPSRs) in 2011. Possible reasons are (1) less experienced junior staff were drafting the reports without sufficient oversight, (2) a larger XPSR program following IFC's portfolio growth over the last five years (77 XPSRs in 2011 compared to 53 XPSRs in 2007), or (3) portfolio staff are also working on new projects that take precedence.

In 2010 IEG started to evaluate separately the quality of the E&S effects section in the XPSRs, using 10 criteria on agreed with IFC's Environmental, Social and Governance Department. This assessment has been submitted to E&S specialists in charge of this section in the XPSR. Consequently, the quality of that section has much improved, from a 33 percent success rate in 2010 to 70 percent in 2011. Improved quality in that section is also reflected in the reduced difference between the XPSR self-evaluation rating and IEG's rating, which was 31 percent in 2010 and

Figure 2.1   Percentage of XPSRs Judged by IEG to Be "Good Practice"

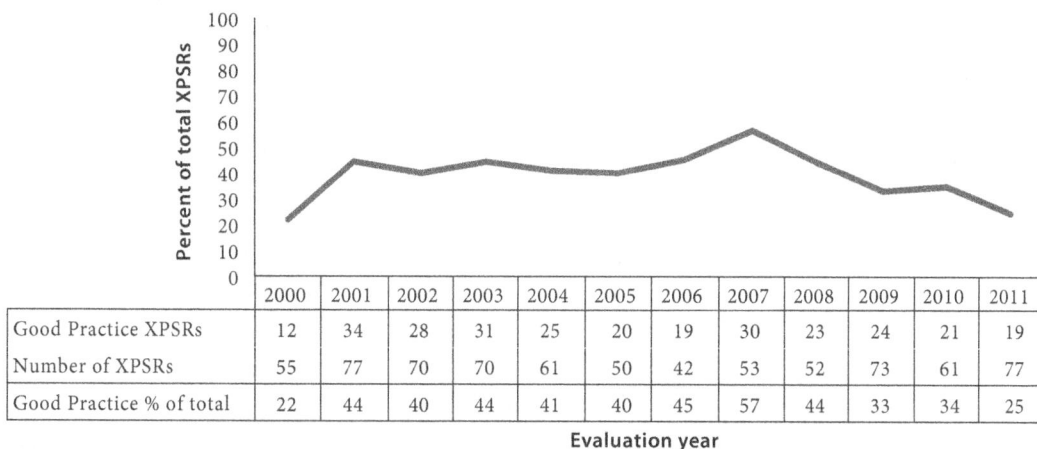

	2000	2001	2002	2003	2004	2005	2006	2007	2008	2009	2010	2011
Good Practice XPSRs	12	34	28	31	25	20	19	30	23	24	21	19
Number of XPSRs	55	77	70	70	61	50	42	53	52	73	61	77
Good Practice % of total	22	44	40	44	41	40	45	57	44	33	34	25

Evaluation year

Source: IEG.

Note: XPSR = Expanded Project Supervision Report.

17 percent in 2011. The rationale to justify the E&S effects rating has improved in particular, from a 44 to 72 percent success rate.

Every XPSR contains the Investment Department's self-ratings for all performance indicators and for overall development outcome. IEG's validations of XPSRs are undertaken to apply independent judgment and to maintain uniformity across IFC, and IEG assigns its own ratings to each projects. IEG's ratings may be higher or lower than those recommended in the XPSR, but on balance they have been lower. IEG's net downward ratings have ranged between 2 and 10 percent over the past 6 years for all rating categories. This bias is common with self-evaluations (IEG 2008, p. 17), but it has widened in the two most recent years.

The success rate is the percentage of ratings that are "Highly Successful," "Successful," or "Mostly Successful" for development outcome and "Excellent" or "Satisfactory" for the other indicators. The average success rates improved gradually until 2009 but declined in 2010 (figure 2.2). IEG measures the disconnect between IFC self-ratings and its own (final) XPSR ratings. The increase in the success rate in 2008 and 2009 has been associated with a corresponding increase in the difference between XPSRs and IEG ratings.[11] There were also significant increases in the last three years in the differences between IFC and IEG ratings on work quality (figure 2.3).

Figure 2.2	Development Outcome Success Rates and Differences between XPSR Self-Evaluation and IEG Rating

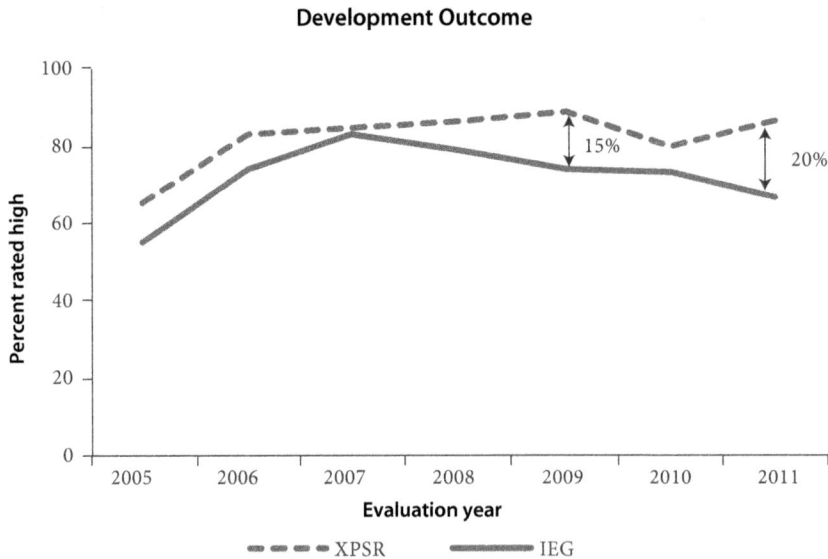

Source: IEG.
Note: XPSR = Expanded Project Supervision Report.

Figure 2.3

Figure 2.3 Work Quality Success Rates and Differences between XPSR Self-Evaluation and IEG Rating

IFC Work Quality

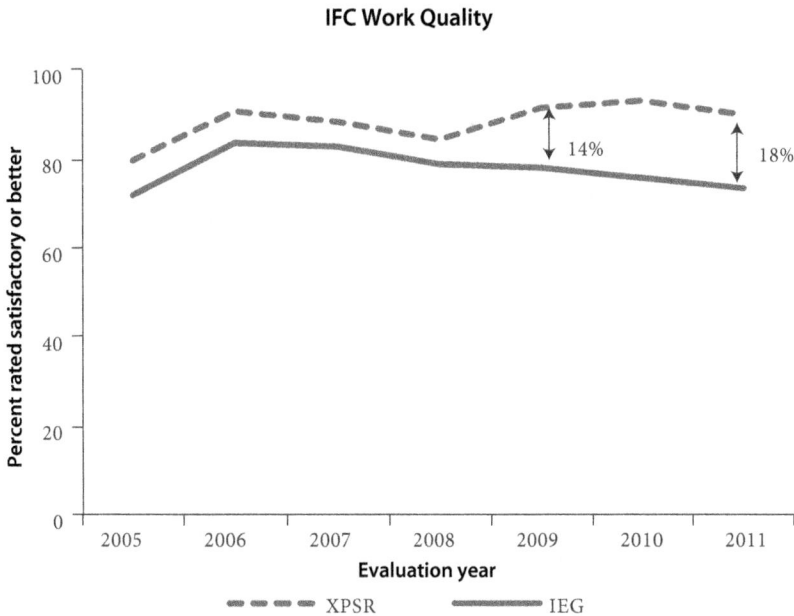

Source: IEG.
Note: XPSR = Expanded Project Supervision Report.

The DOTS ratings for development outcome appear to be more in line with IEG success rates than XPSR self-ratings. DOTS ratings are updated every year. DOTS and XPSRs use similar criteria based on the good practice standards, but XPSR authors tended to give higher ratings than DOTS in 2009 (by 11 percent of DOTS ratings) and 2011 (9 percent) for the same project or company. However, IEG often applied lower ratings—to as much as 22 percent of self-XPSR ratings in the past three years (see table 2.2).

Table 2.2 DOTS, XPSR, and IEG Development Outcome Ratings on Binary Basis (projects with DOTS, XPSR, and IEG ratings)

	2009	2010	2011
DOTS success rate (%)	78	79	78
XPSR success rate (%)	88	79	86
IEG success rate (%)	72	75	67
Number of projects	69	57	64

Source: IEG.
Note: DOTS ratings are at the end June of XPSR evaluation year. XPSR = Expanded Project Supervision Report.

DOTS data are used for internal and external reporting—descriptive statistics, tables, and graphs—for nonfinancial aspects of IFC's operations. Aggregation is the primary form of data analysis. Reports aggregate mandatory indicators by sector, region, and contributions to reach targets, and so forth, to describe portfolio trends. These reports are produced by CDI and underlie annual strategic discussions (see chapter 3).

DOTS development outcome ratings are part of IFC's Development Outcome score. They are aggregated using a six-year rolling average. For example, the 2012 annual report uses investments approved between 2003 and 2008, which are mature enough to be rated and recent enough to be relevant—about 40 percent of active projects. About 45 percent of projects were committed in the last four years and are too young to be reliably assessed. The remaining 15 percent were committed 10 or more years ago and are not necessarily representative of recent investments.

The primary users of M&E information within the operational departments are strategists and economists. Based on the staff survey, about two-thirds of them analyze summary ratings and project indicators for the business, and nearly half of them analyze what works and what does not in their lines of business. Many conduct their own analyses because DOTS data cover a six-year slice of active projects; some clients are not covered after the time horizon, or a project may be closed and no longer monitored in DOTS.

Box 2.2	Evaluation Cooperation Group Benchmarking of IFC's and MIGA's Evaluation Systems

The ECG Working Group on Private Sector Evaluation established good practice standards for evaluation of private sector operations in 2001 and revised them in 2003 and 2006. Their goal is to harmonize evaluation among MDBs. The ECG periodically benchmarks its members relative to the standards, most recently in 2011 when it looked at the private sector operations of eight MDBs.

The report (ECG 2011) noted that IFC met 93 percent of the good practice standards, the highest level of adoption and application among multilaterals. The gap is a result of IFC's not adopting four revised standards with which it disagreed. Three of these involved IFC's rating of additionality as a part of work quality rather than a separate dimension of performance, and one involved the method for assessing the business success of loans to financial intermediaries.

The report found that MIGA met 73 percent of the good practice standards. It is important to note that this assessment was done before the introduction of self-evaluation, thus it refers to IEG's evaluation of MIGA's operations. The major disconnects include that MIGA did not meet the standard relating to sample size (because it would cost too much to evaluate a statistically significant sample) and that MIGA's annual report did not cover all evaluations conducted during the year. The other areas were related to IEG's dissemination of evaluation findings and systematic collection of lessons. In contrast, like IFC, MIGA also does not agree with the additionality standards. MIGA believes the rating should be 82 percent based on the nature of its business, which is different from other international financial institutions that make direct investments.

Source: ECG 2011.

Monitoring and Evaluation for IFC Advisory Services

IFC's Advisory Services provide advice, problem solving, and capacity building to companies, industries, financial institutions, and governments. These services complement IFC's investments, as more than 90 percent of work with private companies is with actual or potential clients. National or local government clients account for around half of the advisory projects. IFC advises them on how to improve their investment climates and how to strengthen infrastructure by working with the private sector.

Advisory Services[12] grew more than tenfold in expenditures and sixfold in staffing between FY01 and FY12. In FY11, the business was structured in four business lines: Access to Finance, Investment Climate, Sustainable Business, and Public-Private Partnerships (PPPs).

MONITORING OF ADVISORY SERVICES PROJECTS

IFC has considerable control over the design and execution of its Advisory Services, and the Advisory Services M&E system is integrated into the project cycle from design to completion.

"AT ENTRY" FOUNDATIONS FOR MONITORING

ASOP, introduced in FY11, is an interactive, online operational system and project control mechanism comparable to DOTS. The cycle begins with a pre-implementation phase, where the project concepts are identified and related to IFC's strategic goals. Each business line has a standard framework that includes indicators for outputs, outcomes, and impacts. These enable IFC to compare projects and aggregate their results. Staff set project targets at one point and for any duration.

Advisory Services has results measurement officers in each business line and in the regions. Their roles, as specified in the operational procedures, are more formal than the DOTS champions. They are required to advise on aspects related to results measurement during the pre-implementation phase. They are also responsible for reviewing data gathering. At project closure, the results measurement officers are required to participate in the Project Completion Report (PCR) review, as well as other project cycle meetings.[13]

IFC has developed standard output, outcome, and impact indicators for all Advisory Services projects. These indicators are tracked from approval through project supervision and completion. The data are used for ongoing project management and corporate reporting. These indicators are incorporated in project documents at the concept review and staff articulate expected outcomes and discuss indicators choices.

IEG validates a sample of Advisory Services PCRs;[14] summary statistics are shown in figure 2.4. At-entry M&E quality has improved over the last three years: there is better use of logical models, relevant indicators, and more baseline data. The incidence of "little or no" has declined and the incidence of "to a great extent"

Figure 2.4   M&E Quality at Entry, 2008–10

Does the project have a good logical framework?

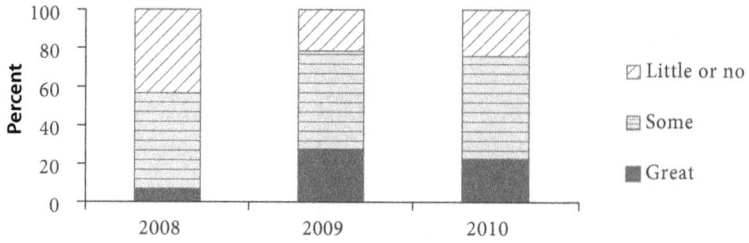

Little or no
Some
Great

Approval document cites relevant baseline data?

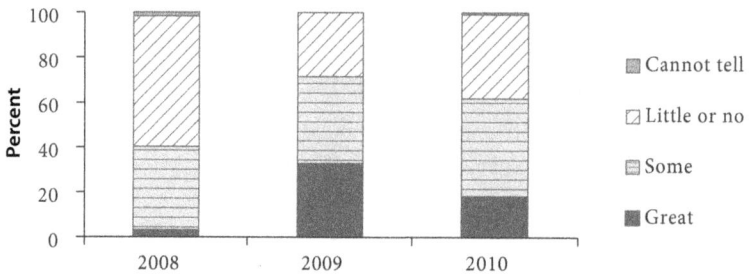

Cannot tell
Little or no
Some
Great

Approval document cites intended indicators for results tracking?

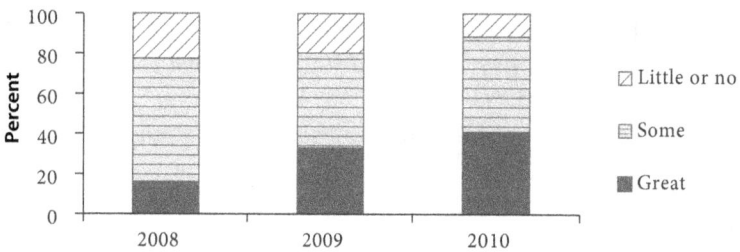

Little or no
Some
Great

Relevant standard indicators used?

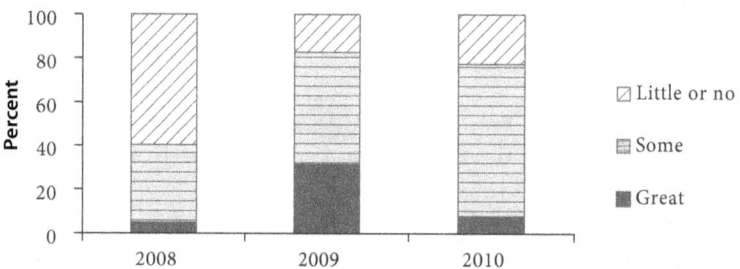

Little or no
Some
Great

Source: IEG.

has increased for all indicators. However, the goal on all these dimensions is to have 100 percent of PCRs rated as "to a great extent," and there are still significant shortfalls. About 80 percent did not meet this standard for logical framework or baseline data; 90 percent fell short on standard indicators; and 60 percent did not cite tracking indicators in approval documents. The use of a budget for pre-implementation activities,[15] including gathering baseline data, contributes to M&E quality at entry. But 40 percent of projects had no baseline data. Moreover, there are instances of problematic baselines—for example, the baselines were not sufficiently representative, or the baseline survey did not ask the right questions or asked leading questions. The new policy gives staff up to a year to collect baseline and other data before the operational start of a project, but the quality of baseline data gathering should be improved.

More projects are using standard indicators. In 2008, nearly 60 percent of projects did not have relevant standard indicators. In 2010, nearly 80 percent had at least some. However, only 10 percent of projects had relevant standard indicators, and some standard indicators were not relevant: they were adopted because they were required. Nonstandard indicators are used to supplement; 65 percent of Advisory Services staff say that standard indicators are not sufficient to track project results, and 53 percent of projects they supervise have other, nonmandatory indicators.

The PSR is the principal monitoring instrument. The first PSR is an opportunity to refine indicators, collect baseline data, and clarify targets. At this stage, data are entered in the ASOP. The PSR is updated semiannually, with the project's status and information about risks to intended objectives. Project ratings are assigned during the PSR cycle on several dimensions such as development results—output, outcomes, and impacts; financial—funding, client cash fees, client additional contributions; implementation—timeline and staffing; and overall rating, based on specific guidelines that were developed with CDI and need management sign-off and discussed in portfolio review meetings. These performance ratings help identify areas of corrective actions if needed.

Data Gathering

Advisory Services' principal sources of data are IFC, client firms and government agencies, and studies and surveys by consultants, national statistics offices, the World Bank, other international agencies, or civil society organizations. According to responses to the staff survey, Advisory Services staff gather data from nonclient sources such as public domain information. About 45 percent of staff sought data from clients; nearly two-thirds sought public domain data and gathered data directly. Staff also look at internal IFC data (60 percent) or third-party data (54 percent).

During supervision, staff identified gaps by reviewing documents (76 percent), having discussions with clients (70 percent) and relevant stakeholders (61 percent), and making field visits (47 percent). PSR updating improved between 2008 and 2010, so only 5 percent of projects had little or no information in supervision reports, 10 percent lacked tracking indicators, and 17 percent had no audit trails for results (see figure 2.5).

Figure 2.5   Project Supervision Documents Quality

Supervision document report on up-to-date project developments?

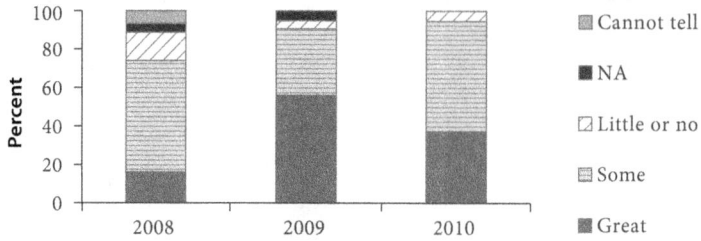

Supervision tracks relevant indicators?

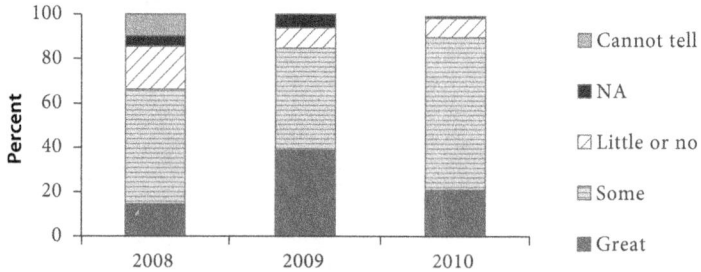

Supervision document provides a coherent audit trail of results?

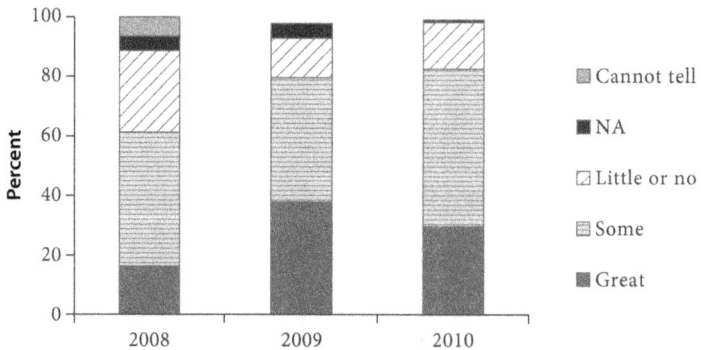

Source: IEG.

QUALITY CONTROL

There are three levels of data quality control: project officers, results measurement officers, and officers in CDI. Project staff is the front line of controlling data quality. Based on the staff survey, they validate data principally by:

- Contacting clients—78 percent
- Consulting with field-based colleagues—70 percent
- Reviewing multiple sources of information—65 percent
- Contacting stakeholders—64 percent

- Conducting site visits—43 percent less than half the time, 25 percent more than half the time, 22 percent always.

The regional business line managers have primary accountability for their results data and the performance ratings. The data quality was checked by project team, their managers, and results measurement specialists. Project teams did their own data quality control; 90 percent of staff have contacted data sources to validate data they have received. Some needed additional clarification; 44 percent of staff who answered the survey reported that they have contacted the data source by checking inconsistency with site visit information. Furthermore, one-third of this additional inquiry was also triggered by the review of M&E specialists.

Results measurement officers are critical in quality control during supervision, and they have a formal role in the PSR. During the semiannual supervision review of projects, managers seek guidance from M&E staff and confirm that results measurement issues have been addressed. Results measurement officers review data entry in the results measurement system. The Results Measurement Network[16] within CDI coordinates evaluation efforts for advisory services across IFC. The network has developed a number of checklists and tools to answer frequently asked questions and to provide guidance to staff, including guidance on proper project documentation for PDS approvals, PSRs, PCRs, and tools to guide cost-benefit analysis.

IFC took steps to improve project documentation by conducting reviews by CDI. Reviews cover all Advisory Services implementation plan documents. The review determined whether the new approvals have well-defined objectives, baselines, and targets for indicators for a sample of projects. It also examined baseline and target data and data quality in a sample of PSRs.

Project Filing and Financial Data Management

Filing of project documents has been an issue. The filing system lacks records of offline project approvals, the minutes of PCR review meetings, off-line approvers' comments, documents that constitute a project output, and documents that provide additional evidence for ratings. During its PCR validations, IEG often found that attachments were missing, particularly those related to external evaluation reports, surveys, and other data that could support the ratings. There is no check for the consistency of data filing.

As a part of the development effectiveness criteria, PCRs assess projects' efficiency in use of resources, whether the resources were expensed economically and resources were reasonable in relation to alternatives. In FY10, management reformed financial management, based on the 2007 pricing policy to strengthen client commitment to implementing reforms and to consider the public benefits of a project to better ensure that any subsidies are warranted based on the degree of public benefits.

However, IEG's early findings based on 140 closed projects approved after the pricing policy was implemented (of which, 81 projects were explicitly expecting some form of contributions) indicate that there have been some difficulties in monitoring client contributions. There were no apparent systemic problems recording actual cash contributions. However, only 8 of 25 projects with expected in-kind contributions at approval recorded actual contributions by closure. Similarly, IFC expected 33 projects to have parallel contributions but only 6 recorded actual contributions by closure. These gaps could be caused by poor recording of parallel and in-kind contributions in the system, making it impossible to verify actual versus expected contributions.

Data gaps appear to be related to migration to a new budget system in FY09 and to a new reporting platform in FY11. As a result, project completion expenses or actual project costs did not match across three data sources (the new system, Advisory Services databases, and PCR data) for some projects. These gaps prevented IEG from conducting a thorough analysis of actual client contributions for those projects and thus assessing the efficiency of resource use in the project. The FY11 rollout of pricing guidance sought to strengthen the role of client contributions, and systems were upgraded to record and monitor contributions through PSRs.

SELF-EVALUATION FOR ADVISORY SERVICES

Project evaluation takes place at completion, based on the PCR, to cover IFC's Advisory Services overall performance. The framework was developed jointly by IFC and IEG in FY06, drawing on the Organisation for Economic Co-operation and Development Advisory Committee's principles of evaluation and IFC's purpose and mission. It was piloted for two years (FY06–07) and has been used for five years. PCRs are required for all Advisory Services projects, unless they were dropped or terminated, and are due within three months of project closure. As with the XPSR system for investment projects, project teams produce the PCRs as the final monitoring report. Unlike XPSRs, which are a random sample, PCRs are mandatory and are produced for all closed projects.

The PCR assesses and assigns ratings for the following dimensions: strategic relevance, output achievement, outcome achievement, impact achievement, and efficiency. These ratings are synthesized into a single development effectiveness rating, on a six-point scale, from highly successful (overwhelmingly positive development results and virtually no flaws) to highly unsuccessful (negative results and no positive aspects to compensate). Furthermore, the PCR contains a rating on IFC's role and contribution, which assesses IFC's additionality to the project. IEG provides a guideline for preparing PCRs, and IEG and IFC are currently working to update that guideline.

After PCRs are completed, CDI reviews them to determine whether the project team's self-ratings are supported by evidence and conform to IFC's M&E framework. The department assigns its own project ratings, which become the official IFC rating for all reporting, including IFC's annual report. These ratings have been entered in ASOP since FY11.

IEG assesses project success and the quality of documentation and summarizes its views and ratings in an Evaluative Note (EvNote). IEG began validations in

FY08. It validated all PCRs in FY08 and FY09 and a sample of PCRs starting in FY10.[17] IEG reviews a random sample (51 percent three-year rolling average) of projects closed in the previous fiscal year. IEG's assessment is a desk review of project documents and other sources including any external evaluations. IEG also makes selective field validations.

The quality of PCRs has improved from a low base (figure 2.6). PCRs have sharply increased the number of lessons for future operations. However, there is room for improvement in using baseline information. In 2010 about one-third of PCRs were making little or no use of baseline data, and another 40 percent of PCRs had shortcomings in baseline information provided.[18]

Measuring the achievement of outcomes and impacts of IFC Advisory Services has been challenging. PCRs increasingly contain information to justify ratings for strategic relevance, achievement of outputs, efficiency, and IFC's role and contribution; yet only one-third contain sufficient information to justify their development effectiveness ratings (see figure 2.7). Even after some improvement, nearly a quarter of PCRs had not met a minimum standard for information and justification to support outcome achievement ratings, and another 46 percent had shortcomings in information and justification for ratings. For impact ratings, half the PCRs did not contain adequate evidence to support the rating. The data issues in the PCR that are not sufficient to assess performance are generally the following:

- Use of estimates as close proxy of actual results or key inputs in computation that claims outcome and impacts

- Attributing impacts even though actual impacts are too far removed from project activities; or attributing more impacts than are warranted from IFC's share of the financing

- Attributing outcomes or impacts that are not part of the projects' objectives or activities.

IEG found that outcome and impact discussions could be improved by developing contextual analyses (such as trend analysis, discussion of externalities, counterfactual scenarios, and discussion of results versus baseline and evidence of the project's attribution to increase over the baseline, as compared to previous years' growth trends) to support the quantitative data. These analyses would provide a more credible attribution-oriented understanding of the project's results and achievements.

IEG independently rated development effectiveness, upgrading 8 percent of the ratings and downgrading 19 percent (2008–10 PCRs). Over the three years, IEG verified 46 percent of PCR ratings, downgrading 19 percent and upgrading 8 percent. IEG also assigned "too early to judge" (TETJ) and "cannot verify" (CV) where results were not yet apparent or where the data in the PCR were insufficient to determine a rating.[19] CDI also reviews PCRs and assigns independent ratings, and CDI's ratings are used in the corporate performance records. CDI and IEG ratings were constantly lower than the original PCR self-ratings (see figure 2.8). It is important to note that IEG does not validate CDI's ratings, and that CDI's ratings are not formally integrated in the PCR self-evaluation system documents. IEG's validation is formal process involving written records of validation (EvNote) and detailed justification that justifies rating differences from the original PCR. This is performed with some time lag after the PCR's finalization and often benefits from additional information and in some instances field visits. CDI reviews do not have detailed records of justification of rating changes.

Figure 2.6 — PCR Information Quality

Uses baseline data appropriately?
Legend: Cannot tell, Little or no, Some, Great

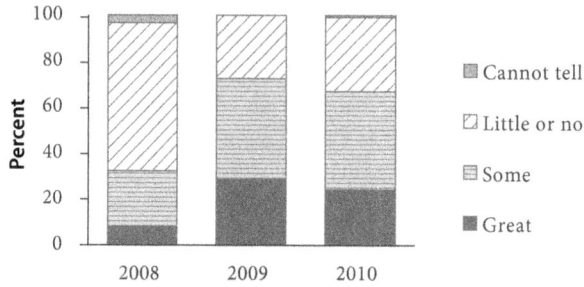

Discusses results of all program components?
Legend: Little or no, Some, Great

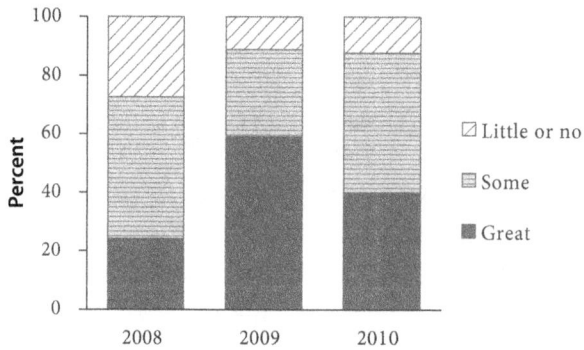

Contains useful and well-structured lessons?
Legend: Little or no, Some, Great

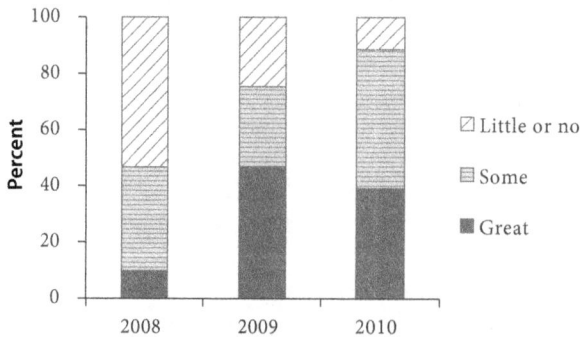

Source: IEG.
Note: PCR = Project Completion Report.

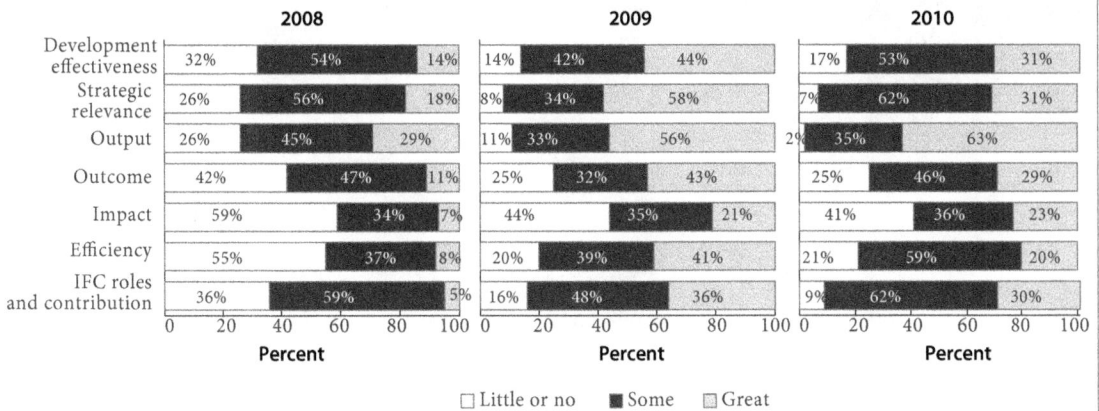

Figure 2.7 — Adequacy of Information to Justify Ratings

	2008			2009			2010		
Development effectiveness	32%	54%	14%	14%	42%	44%	17%	53%	31%
Strategic relevance	26%	56%	18%	8%	34%	58%	7%	62%	31%
Output	26%	45%	29%	11%	33%	56%	2%	35%	63%
Outcome	42%	47%	11%	25%	32%	43%	25%	46%	29%
Impact	59%	34%	7%	44%	35%	21%	41%	36%	23%
Efficiency	55%	37%	8%	20%	39%	41%	21%	59%	20%
IFC roles and contribution	36%	59%	5%	16%	48%	36%	9%	62%	30%

Percent — Percent — Percent

☐ Little or no   ■ Some   ☐ Great

Source: IEG.

In the earlier years, there were large fluctuations among PCR self, CDI and IEG ratings (see figure 2.8). They were caused by factors such as changes in operational arrangements (structure, leadership, and key personnel) and the fact that the system itself is less mature than the one for Investments, and Advisory Services staff are still gaining experience with it. Although over the three-year average (FY08–10) the disconnect between IEG and PCR ratings was 12 percent, the gap is considerably less between IEG and CDI, at 1 percent. As the system becomes more mature, one might expect a more consistent approach for rating to evolve across PCRs, CDI, and possibly IEG; yet this would need to be assessed on a continual basis in the future.

Over the entire FY08–10 review period, IEG could not assign development effectiveness ratings to 18 percent of projects selected for evaluation. In most instances (65 percent of the cases) this was a result of insufficient achievement in outcomes, making it impossible to assign a development effectiveness rating by completion. Sometimes there was evidence of clear momentum and a likelihood that with a bit more time results may emerge. In other incidences (35 percent), inability to rate development effectiveness was a result of insufficient information and lack of credible evidence in the PCR to justify the development effectiveness rating. Note that IEG assigns development effectiveness largely based on achievement of outcomes.[20] Moreover, even among those for which IEG assigned development effectiveness ratings, 41 percent could not be rated at the impact level because impacts had not been observed by evaluation/project closure or because there was insufficient information and evidence to assign a rating.

Although there was general agreement between PCRs and IEG among the ratings for strategic relevance, output achievement, and IFC's role and contribution, there was only about 30 percent agreement between PCRs and IEG on impact ratings. One factor contributing to the differences on impact ratings is that IEG changed

Figure 2.8

PCR Self-Rating, CDI and IEG Ratings (development effectiveness ratings) for Subset of Projects Having Three Different Rating Sources (PCR self ratings, CDI and IEG) on Binary Basis

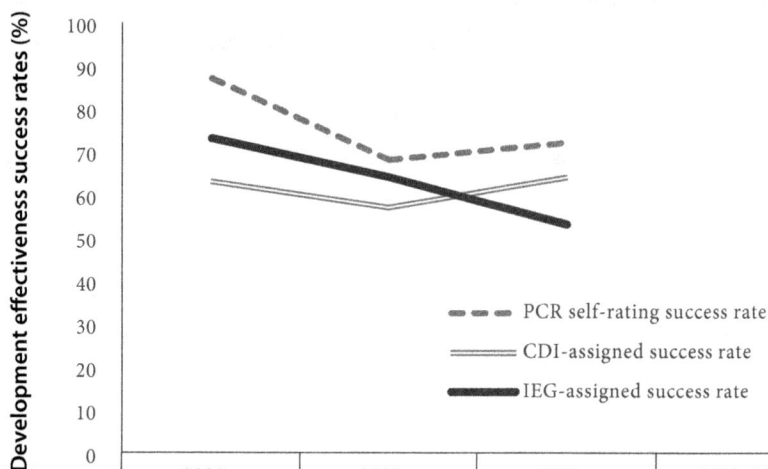

	2008	2009	2010	2008–10
PCR self-rating success rate (%)	87	68	72	73
CDI-assigned success rate (%)	63	57	64	60
IEG-assigned success rate (%)	73	64	53	61
PCR self-rating vs. CDI (%)	−24	−11	−8	−13
PCR self-rating vs. IEG (%)	−14	−4	−19	−12
CDI vs. IEG (%)	10	7	−11	1
Number of PCRs	30	76	78	184

Y-axis: Development effectiveness success rates (%)

Legend:
- - - PCR self-rating success rate
—— CDI-assigned success rate
━━ IEG-assigned success rate

Source: IEG.

Note: CDI = Development Impact Department; PCR = Project Completion Report. They are a subset of PCRs with both CDI and IEG ratings and do not represent the portfolio.

many ratings to TETJ or CV. IEG assigned TETJ when it was too soon to make a concrete judgment on impact achievements. CV reflected poor PCR quality and indicated inadequate PCR information or analyses for IEG to assign a rating. Nearly 17 percent of projects rated positively for impact were modified by IEG to either CV (14 percent of all) or TETJ (9 percent). Similarly, IEG reclassified about 7 percent of projects rated positive in outcome achievement to TETJ, and another 7 percent to CV.

The CV designation indicates that the data in the PCR are not sufficient to assess performance. For example, in the Sustainable Business Advisory business line, IEG rated 45 percent of all PCRs that were eligible to have impact ratings[21] in FY10 and found 40 percent of them had CV rating because of insufficient data and analysis or a lack of survey or credible data collection among clients. Only 14 percent of them were rated TETJ.

For investment climate projects, IEG rated 52 percent of all impact eligible projects reviewed in FY10, 38 percent as TETJ and only 10 percent as CV because of insufficient data and analysis. For the Access to Finance business line, IEG has been assessing the impact based on sustainable contributions made at the financial institution level and assessing impacts on beneficiaries beyond the financial intermediary clients as possible,[22] given that the existing approach to assessing impact, including the IFC standard core impact indicator, at the business line level has been largely inadequate. Using this approach, IEG was able to rate impact in 44 percent of all impact eligible projects in FY10. In contrast, 47 percent was rated TETJ —given that many access to finance projects were linked to IFC investments, data availability was less of a problem and only 6 percent could not be rated because of insufficient evidence (CV).

MEASURING LONGER-TERM IMPACTS

IEG notes that for the most part, IFC "impact" indicators are more like "final outcomes" in the World Bank and other MDB frameworks, rather than broad longer-term impacts. For example, a main impact indicator for investment climate projects is private sector savings from business reforms. This is simply a quantification of time and money saved from new government procedures captured under outcomes. In PCRs reviewed, the number was often based on calculation estimates without a survey to see how many businesses had undergone the new process.

For Sustainable Business Advisory projects, a main impact indicator is sales revenue enhancements gained by adopting practice recommended by the project and collected by a survey or estimated by the team. Without a survey or some robust data and reliance on estimates, the claims in PCRs frequently do not have sufficient basis. In contrast, longer-term impact indicators are used in PPPs, for which impacts attempt to capture public sector fiscal savings and beneficiaries of the new or improved services introduced by the PPP and they are for the most part not observable by PCR. For Access to Finance, the main "impact" indicator is "value of financing facilitated," which often overlaps with ones of the main outcome indicators (value of loans disbursed), has been problematic in its interpretation across IFC projects reviewed, and was often not aligned with project objectives.

Many PCRs stated that a post-completion survey needed to be conducted; however, there has been no formal, systematic follow-up after the PCR. So far, there were either ad hoc or selective postcompletion initiatives or external evaluations, for example, in the PPP business line's tracking of postimplementation activities for projects that successfully closed PPP transactions, and the Middle East and North Africa Region's exercise of data collection for projects closed in previous years. However, they lacked systematic ways to gather postcompletion data and did not adequately cover the IFC's Advisory Services portfolio. Moreover, neither IEG nor CDI has a system to verify those findings.

Determining the timing and scope of either a more mature point in time to conduct self-evaluation or to conduct postcompletion follow-up could be based on past projects' tendencies and results achievement patterns. With the exception of PPP projects, IEG's assessment of FY08–10 projects suggests that two to three years after completion would be reasonable. For example, for Access to Finance projects, data gathering is neither costly nor difficult, as impacts should be observable within two years of project completion. IEG analysis shows that most greenfield microfinance institutions and transition projects take longer than gender or SME banking projects to achieve their objectives, for example. For Sustainable Business Advisory projects, impacts should be monitorable earlier on given their nature and objectives (typically enhanced farmer or SME sales revenues or income), but many of these projects also require some type of survey to collect data to show results.

Investment climate reforms take time to implement, but two years postcompletion should be sufficient for most IFC investment climate projects. Like Sustainable Business Advisory, some investment climate project types (namely business regulation streamlining) would require some form of survey to determine cost savings to the private sector. PPP projects have a longer time horizon than the other business lines and impacts can only be measured after the PPPs have been implemented, which often involves construction and can take three or more years before being operational.

One reason for gaps in capturing outcomes and impacts was the use of objectives that are not achievable by the time of project closure. Since FY10, Advisory Services has revised its project objective setting approach to determine what is achievable within the project timeframe and budget and has stated that it aims to capture intermediate project results. IEG has looked at a few of the new project objective approaches in recent projects, and many of them are setting two targets for outcomes and impact—one at project completion and tracked in PCRs, and another at three to five years later to capture IDGs.

One concern about this approach is that it sets targets achievable at the time of project's early operating history or delivery without other follow-up mechanisms covering longer-term achievements, and that may create gaps in evaluation scope. Another concern is about the creation of a system whereby longer-term outcome and impact achievement are measured outside IFC's regular self-evaluation process and outside of the scope of IEG's validation program. Because IEG has not yet evaluated projects subject to the revised approach, it is not possible to verify that self-evaluations will be better position to capture appropriate outcomes and impacts of the projects.

IFC has been preparing for a more systematic postcompletion follow-up by proposing a postimplementation monitoring system. It is important to maintain focus on adequately tracking achievement of projects' expected outcome and impacts, as reflected by project objectives and goals, regardless of whether that happens at completion or a couple of years later. Moreover, these postcompletion follow-up measures should have clear selection criteria for projects to be allowed to remain active for longer periods. The system should also have clear institutional and budget allocation for credible execution with a mechanism for a quality control. Also, the results measurement matrix should contain appropriate quantitative targets for postcompletion to be judged. In addition, to prevent the above mentioned concerns, the approach and results must lend themselves for systematic validation by IEG, so as to ensure consistency of the entire evaluation structure.

METHODS OF DATA ANALYSIS

During execution, monitoring checks progress against the expected outcomes and impacts. Various flags are used to identify potential issues. The survey conducted for this evaluation found that nearly two-thirds of the operational staff used M&E to make adjustments. The changes were prompted by discussions with supervisors (62 percent), by noticing project information (55 percent), and by discussions with clients (46 percent).

Results measurement officers are the principal analysts of evaluation information. Eighty percent analyze summary ratings, project indicators, and what worked and what did not in their business lines. More than 80 percent assessed or summarized the development performance of projects or their business areas (sector, region, business line, and so forth), relying extensively on M&E information. In these assessments, more than 80 percent always used the PSR and/or PCR, and 40 percent always used external evaluations commissioned by IFC; another 20 percent referred to the documents more than half the time.

IFC avoids conflicts of interest by not taking Advisory Services roles and investment roles at the same time with a client for projects in PPP. Partly because of the policy that restricts staff access to internal information outside the business line, Advisory Services staff do not use investment-side information, such as DOTS and XPSRs, and they do not know where these instruments are in IFC's information technology platform. About half did not know where to find DOTS information, and only 20 percent knew the location of XPSRs. Nevertheless, in the Access to Finance and Sustainable business lines, advisory clients are often IFC investment clients, and joint operations are encouraged to provide better service.

For purposes of analysis, the PCR is to a large extent a timely instrument. Sixty-six percent of results measurement officers said they found PCRs always timely, and more than 80 percent found the evaluation reports commissioned by IFC timely more than half the time.

Thematic Evaluations at IFC

Since 2005, Advisory Services has been conducting several types of evaluations: external project evaluations, including rapid outcome evaluations; effectiveness audit or impact evaluations; program-level evaluations; and business line or regional facility evaluations. Recently, CDI consolidated the data of these thematic evaluations. There were 123 evaluations since 2005, of which half (66) were impact evaluations. There have been extensive thematic evaluations of Advisory Services, but very few of IFC investment activities until recently. This is because external evaluations are often useful to improve Advisory Services products and take them through the "development stage" and give them legitimacy to further demonstrate the business case.

The thematic evaluations mainly respond to management's needs to inform strategies and operations or to donor requests. IEG reviewed 26 impact evaluations (IEG 2012) and found that they were often led by Advisory Services staff based on availability of funding, project team, or donor interest, without a strategic selection framework. However, there is a trend for regional facilities and business lines to be more actively involved in evaluations.

Most evaluations were conducted by external experts, managed by IFC M&E specialists. IEG's staff survey found that more than half of Advisory Services staff who worked on project preparation never consulted externally commissioned evaluations of IFC's projects. These evaluations were not well coordinated within IFC, and records and reports could not be easily located in IFC's archives. The difficulties of using archives might have contributed to staff's relatively low use of thematic evaluations.

The same review of impact evaluation by IEG (2012) found that about half the impact evaluations were of medium or high quality. The main limitations of the low-quality impact evaluations were small samples and weak evaluation designs.

IFC's Evaluation Strategy

IFC adopted an evaluation strategy in FY12, with the goal of having a more focused approach to evaluation across the Corporation. The strategy emphasizes learning from all projects: what worked, what didn't, why, and how. It is intended to employ thematic and programmatic evaluation to improve evaluation and close knowledge gaps and to develop business cases to link advisory services with investment operations. The findings are expected to provide business insights for better services to clients and partners. Furthermore, evaluation is expected to articulate the impact of IFC's work, especially on poverty and economic growth.

Corporate Monitoring and Evaluation

Starting in FY07, DOTS scores (the percentage of ratings that were mostly successful or better) for investment projects were featured in IFC's scorecard, replacing the scores from XPSRs. In FY12, the development effectiveness score was introduced for Advisory Services as another scorecard item, based on ratings from CDI. In addition to the DOTS scores, the scorecard also tracks volume of investment commitments and advisory project expenditures in focus areas such as Africa, the Middle East and North Africa, IDA countries, or focus sectors or themes (South-South projects) as indicators for "greater development impacts."

In 2011, IFC introduced IDGs—targets for reach, access, or other outcomes that reflect clients' increased contributions in priority areas. They are intended to complement the existing results framework and to infuse IFC's strategic and operational decisions with greater attention to development results. After two years of piloting, two of the IDGs (Health and Educational Services and Financial Services) will go live in FY13.

The six IDGs are—

1: Increase or improve sustainable farming opportunities.

2: Improve health and education services.

3a: Increase access to financial services for micro/individual clients.

3b: Increase access to financial services for SME clients.

4: Increase or improve infrastructure services.

5: Contribute to economic growth (value added).

6: Reduce greenhouse gas emissions.

The IDGs have three notable features. First, data are taken from existing M&E systems wherever possible, using existing indicators. Second, IDGs are ex ante indicators based on reach from new—not existing—projects. Third, they are based on expectations at entry, with initial targets expressed over five years.

Another difference between expected reach numbers and IDGs is the application of a "contribution rule." IFC is interested in measuring the incremental reach in relation to its financing. For example, if IFC's equity investment is 10 percent or more of project cost, 100 percent of incremental reach is attributed to IFC, but if it is less than 10 percent, then a prorated, incremental reach is counted.

Although the introduction of corporate goals based on a development footprint is important, there are several issues in IDGs.

- Implicit targets are volume driven. There may be a bias toward large-scale projects that generate large IDG numbers, or toward projects in populous countries and regions without reference to beneficiaries' poverty levels.

- They are weak in attributing reach to IFC's contribution. Several IDGs use IFC's share in financing as a rule of attributing to IFC. Although there is an emphasis on taking conservative numbers, it does not have sufficient grounds to claim IFC's role in achieving client companies' reach.

- There is no reference to counterfactuals (what conditions would be without IFC intervention); thus, they are not indicating impacts to the society.

- Quality control of data is more important, especially when the IDGs are now linked to management incentive systems.

- Given the strong emphasis on IDGs in IFC's business decisions, there is a risk that they lead to misalignment of incentives. For example, staff might focus on measuring large reach numbers for IDGs rather than paying attention to delivering meaningful impact that IFC projects could bring to people and society.

IFC undertook an extensive consultations and testing over several years before adding the IDGs to the Corporate Scorecard. And an IDG is only one measure and is supplemented by others such as commitment volume and numbers in IDA countries. IDGs use the client company (investment) or project team (advisory services) to provide ex ante indicators and data during supervision. The data's quality is checked by documentation reviews, as they are processed in the existing M&E systems.

Monitoring and Evaluation in MIGA

Business Model of MIGA and Monitoring and Evaluation

MIGA is in the business of political risk guarantees. It sells noncommercial risk mitigation products to foreign investors—unlike IFC, which helps to finance firms—and has a substantively different business relationship with its clients. IFC's investment outcome is largely driven by firms' commercial success, but MIGA's is less dependent on this factor. A financier will only get repaid if a firm succeeds, but an insurer is prepaid and is not affected by a firm's commercial success. In political risk insurance, business success is driven by political choices within developing countries.

MIGA, as a development institution and a member of the World Bank Group, has to balance its commercial and development goals in its M&E. Because MIGA's exposure is to certain political risk events, its business needs may not require monitoring of a project's commercial operations. However, it is often difficult to separate commercial from political risks, as various types of risks tend to be correlated as in the case of breach of contract coverage. Correspondingly, more and more commercial insurers tend to look beyond narrowly defined political risks into commercial aspects of the activities they tend to insure.

As a development institution, MIGA is accountable for meeting its development mandate and for minimizing reputational risks to the Bank Group, so its M&E need not strictly follow the practices of commercial insurers but does need to go into areas that help MIGA assess its development impact. It is also accountable for spending its budget wisely, and M&E can be costly. MIGA's underwriting guidelines state that underwriting is to address not only specific political risks for which MIGA may provide insurance, but also assesses risk to the overall financial viability of the project. Also, the guidelines require MIGA to assess a project's anticipated development impact on stakeholders. The development and E&S impacts may have direct impact on the overall assessment of the risk associated with a project.

Unlike IFC, MIGA does not have a fully fledged project supervision function and it has been developing its M&E from scratch under cost constraints but with the advantage of learning from other, more advanced development evaluation paradigms. As MIGA tries to demonstrate its development effects, to fulfill the common purpose as a part of the World Bank Group, and as each project guarantee is justified by its relevance to the country's development goal, certain information is needed to assess whether the projects' development effects MIGA is claiming to have achieved actually materialized.

Under the constraints of its business model, the M&E system in MIGA has evolved over the past 10 years. MIGA established an independent evaluation function in 2002, charged with conducting evaluations of MIGA guarantees. IEG has been the main source of evaluative evidence on MIGA's performance for most of the intervening period. MIGA subsequently created an Economic and Policy Group and the Environmental and Social unit to strengthen the analysis of development impact and E&S issues of MIGA projects.

Recent initiatives signal MIGA's stronger commitment with M&E. It appointed an advisor whose sole responsibility is to coordinate and manage the self-evaluation system. It piloted a self-evaluation system for guarantee projects in FY10 and revised underwriting guidelines to align with self-evaluation requirements. It also strengthened aspects of project monitoring in E&S, and introduced tracking of project development indicators.

MONITORING IN MIGA

MIGA has strengthened components of its project monitoring, although it does not systematically monitor all aspects of performance of its portfolio of guarantee projects. MIGA has a monitoring strategy to track its clients' compliance with E&S safeguards, but it does not systematically follow up on projects' development indicators or other project parameters. As is the practice of its peers in the political risk insurance industry, MIGA had limited knowledge of project developments and results.

MIGA faces considerable challenges in collecting project information because as an insurer it has a more detached relationship—commercially and contractually— with the project than an investor would have. Based on the business practice of political risk guarantees, the enterprises have limited obligations to provide information directly to MIGA unless specified in the contract of guarantee. As a result, MIGA often does not receive regular information about the project company's operations. In addition, in cases where the guarantee contract specifies submission of project updates on E&S, follow-up by MIGA has been weak (IEG 2013, p. 35).

There are two notable new initiatives: the E&S performance monitoring and the new DEIS to implement cost-effective M&E and results tracking systems. IEG will assess their effectiveness in future project and corporate evaluations.

ENVIRONMENTAL AND SOCIAL PERFORMANCE MONITORING

MIGA's E&S policies and guidelines are similar to IFC's, including the 2007 performance standards. MIGA is required to categorize projects at the early stage of appraisal and to assess potential E&S effects. This requires that applicable performance standards—along with other E&S requirements—be included in the Contract of Guarantee so that the project enterprise will meet the E&S

requirements. The Contract of Guarantee contains requirements for other information that must be submitted to MIGA. The legal requirements include formal reporting requirements, similar to IFC's, but only the guarantee holder can require the project enterprise to comply with MIGA's E&S requirements. This does not expose MIGA to additional risk and does not affect MIGA's mediating role either. However, despite the reporting requirements stipulated in the Contract of Guarantee, MIGA has unevenly followed up or requested the reports from the guarantee holders.

MIGA uses risk-based E&S monitoring, placing heavier weight on category A projects (those with the highest perceived risk) and visiting those most frequently. Lower-risk projects (category B or C) or financial intermediaries are monitored less frequently. MIGA's follow-up with guarantee holders regarding the submission of Annual Monitoring Reports or information on the Social and Environmental Management System has been inconsistent.

Detailed assessments of E&S project performance are undertaken for projects selected for self-evaluation or direct evaluation by IEG[23] when staff collect current project information from various sources, including site visits. In 2011, MIGA approved a new E&S monitoring strategy that included a framework and a budget covering most MIGA projects. This broadened E&S monitoring, which had focused mainly on complex projects. MIGA is implementing this program and has added new staff. Consequently, there are more examples of following up on E&S requirements specified in the Contract of Guarantee (IEG 2013, p. 151).

Nevertheless, MIGA did not comprehensively track the E&S effects of all its projects. Of 26 project evaluations in FY10–12, IEG found there were seven cases of insufficient follow-up on E&S documentation and monitoring reports (IEG 2013, p. 151).

THE DEVELOPMENT EFFECTIVENESS INDICATOR SYSTEM

MIGA introduced DEIS in FY11 to compile information on its projects' standardized development impacts and for periodic reporting to the Audit Committee. Before this, IEG's independent project evaluations were the only reports on MIGA's development impacts.

The main function of DEIS is to collect and eventually report on six indicators that are applicable to most projects. They are dollar amounts or numbers for:

- Investment mobilized
- Taxes and fees paid
- Locally procured goods and services
- Training expenditures
- Direct employment
- Community development outlays.

These six indicators are supplemented by sector-specific indicators. For example, power generation projects need data for incremental power outputs in megawatt hours/year and the number of estimated incremental customers.

DEIS collects data at the time of underwriting and three years after the guarantee was issued. Underwriters and risk management officers are responsible for collecting and validating the initial data. The data become part of the underwriting document and are referenced in the Board paper. Subsequently, a DEIS annex is added to the Contract of Guarantee, requiring clients to update the indicators in three years. Guarantee contracts issued after July 1, 2010 (FY11) have an annex that requires the guarantee holders to submit DEIS information. Thereafter, clients are required to submit DEIS information to MIGA.

A review of MIGA projects found less than half of the sampled contracts signed after July 1, 2010 (17 contracts covering 15 projects) contained an annex and data reporting requirement. The reason was that the contract negotiations were already well under way when DEIS was adopted and the new procedures were not introduced into negotiations with clients. All the Contracts of Guarantee issued since then have contained the annex.

MIGA has not collected all mandatory indicators for all projects, so DEIS data at the underwriting stage cannot fully function as a baseline. Among the projects underwritten in FY12, 87 percent had data on direct employment, but the five other mandatory indicators were completed to lesser extents. Data on investment leverage and taxes and fees were collected for 69 percent and 64 percent of projects, respectively; data on locally procured goods were collected from 26 percent, and 10 percent of projects had data for community investment. The missing data are to be expected, as some indicators are not relevant to all projects. For example, data for community investment are relevant for extractive industries projects that spend heavily on community programs, but not necessarily for general manufacturing or financial institutions.

It is premature to evaluate DEIS, as data on results will begin to be collected from FY14. As MIGA gains experience in gathering data, it can modify its approach according to the lessons it learns, while adjusting expectations as appropriate.

There are two issues confronting the DEIS. One is about the cancellation of contracts before the third anniversary of the guarantee. Although MIGA's average period of guarantee is currently about six to seven years, a fraction of guarantees cancelled before the third anniversary. Without an active Contract of Guarantee, MIGA does not have any recourse to gather DEIS data from these clients.

The second issue relates to new MIGA products introduced through the amendments of MIGA's Operational Regulations and Convention in 2010 and 2011, respectively, to offer new products and expanded coverage to insure certain types of existing investments and offer stand-alone debt coverage. Some of these new products will pose challenges for M&E. For example, the nonhonoring of sovereign financial obligation coverage would require a different evaluation methodology because it assesses the sovereign's ability to comply with its financial obligation and not the enterprise itself. Also, there is an inherent challenge to assessing the financial viability or development impact of guarantees supporting existing investments, or portfolios of investments, or for capital market transactions. Furthermore, the relationship between MIGA's guarantee holder and the underlying project becomes potentially more tenuous for new types of coverage, when the risk of nonpayment of construction loans is guaranteed. These guarantees have a finite duration, thus limiting MIGA's leverage to obtain project information. MIGA's existing indicators might not be well suited to these products.

MIGA SELF-EVALUATION

IEG has independently evaluated MIGA guarantee projects since FY03 using quantitative and qualitative benchmarks in a framework similar to that for IFC investments. IEG has drawn random samples of 50 percent of MIGA's guarantee projects. IEG's direct evaluations have typically included site visits, and it produced Project Evaluation Reports (PERs). With close collaboration and consultation with IEG, MIGA introduced self-evaluation in FY10 and has committed to more systematic self-evaluations.

In 2010, before the introduction of self-evaluation, the ECG's Working Group on Private Sector Evaluation benchmarked its members' systems relative to its good practice standards, based on IEG's evaluation activities. MIGA was at a 73 percent level of adoption and application. This was at the same level as in 2004 but higher than in 2002 (23 percent), and well below IFC's more mature system (93 percent). However, it is close to the overall compliance score among eight participants (78 percent) and higher than the Asian Development Bank and the African Development Bank (65 percent and 64 percent, respectively).

MIGA disagreed with the benchmark study on four standards[24] and did not adopt them. In addition, MIGA fell short of the requirements for four standards relating to annual review of evaluation results. In particular, the pool of evaluated guarantees is not sufficient to comply with the standard, which requires it to be statistically representative of the portfolio at the 95 percent confidence level. MIGA explained that because of the size of its portfolio, compliance would imply a near 100 percent coverage each year for several years.

MIGA has piloted self-evaluation and is mainstreaming the system. Self-evaluations are conducted by operational staff rather than contracted out in order to emphasize learning. IEG independently validates MIGA self-evaluations, based on guidelines developed together with MIGA. In addition, in a transition phase, IEG continues to independently evaluate a sample of guarantee projects.

Since FY10, MIGA has conducted 17 self-evaluations: 37 MIGA staff have participated, including 12 of 14 current underwriters and all E&S specialists and economists. MIGA included the self-evaluations among its business deliverables in the annual work program and budget and in staff annual work plans and staff annual objectives.

MIGA staff who participated in the self-evaluation pilot were overwhelmingly positive about their learning. Only 10 percent of respondents in an IEG staff survey did not answer positively. The benefits cited were better understanding of projects' development impacts or risks to development outcomes and improved knowledge of MIGA's policies and procedures. About half the respondents said they have applied the learning in new underwriting.

Staff also cited challenges in data gathering and lack of information on clients as an issue that made financial and economic returns estimation time consuming and imprecise. Moreover, MIGA has to spend extra time and resources to gather and analyze information beyond what the client can or should provide (for example, overall market information), and MIGA does not have in-house capacity to routinely gather and analyze such information. Staff are needed to interpolate data from limited information. Some staff also commented in the survey that the self-evaluation guidelines are not adapted well to MIGA's business model. MIGA and IEG established a working group to address the matter in the context of new Good Practice.

Among players in the political risk insurance market, monitoring of contract compliance by agency staff is not a common practice. Based on a survey of 15 political risk insurance players and MIGA (Gordon 2008), only half (including MIGA) have an explicit mechanism to conduct compliance follow-ups (Gordon 2008, pp. 121–2). Among these, only Overseas Private Investment Cooperation (OPIC–USA), Export Finance and Insurance Corporation (EFIC–Australia), and MIGA explicitly mention conducting onsite inspections (p. 101). However, these inspections are focused on E&S areas and do not address development impacts of host country. In fact, among the 15 players, only 3—Compagnie Française d'Assurance (COFACE–France), PricewaterhouseCoopers AG (PwC–Germany), and OPIC—assess host country development impact as part of their economic evaluation (p. 119). The study concluded that the "general impression left by the survey of the 16 agencies' performance reporting practices is that these are not generally geared to holding the programs accountable for their host country development impacts" (p. 106).

It is important to note that the there are market players that gather data from their clients that may compare MIGA's current practice. In the report, OPIC monitors the actual economic impact of every project until the conclusion of investment. OPIC has two procedures: one is site monitoring, with OPIC randomly selecting the projects that staff will monitor during a three-year period, and the second is the operation of a "self-monitoring" program by which investors complete an annual questionnaire reporting on the project's development impact.

DATA GATHERING

As noted above, MIGA faces challenges in obtaining project company data, but even basic project underwriting records have been difficult for MIGA to locate. Since FY03, IEG has faced considerable challenges in obtaining MIGA documents needed for project evaluations. The situation is the same when IEG validates

MIGA's self-evaluation documents. IEG was unable to locate some at-approval project documents for 5 of 13 validations of MIGA self-evaluations. Furthermore, 7 of 26 projects with IEG ex post evaluations completed in FY10–12 lacked project documents directly relating to the risks MIGA is covering (IEG 2013, p. 151). MIGA has a new system in place to systematically archive documents but the system does not yet fully cover past projects. With incomplete documentation, it was difficult to make concrete judgments on MIGA's work.

When projects are selected for evaluation, the PER provides for a detailed assessment of performance. The staff conducting the evaluation are required to collect the *updated* project information from various sources, especially from the project enterprise, through a site visit arranged in cooperation with the guarantee holder. Most of the 13 self-evaluations validated by IEG included site visits. However, lack of client reporting caused problems in assessing E&S performance. Because of that, IEG concluded that it could not fully assess the E&S performance for about 40 percent of PERs (9 of 23 PERs for which that assessment should be done[25]), including 2 of 13 self-evaluations.

QUALITY CONTROL

For FY10–11, IEG validates the content and recommends adjustments to ratings, as necessary. There are modest differences in ratings between MIGA's self-evaluations and IEG's validation: of 63 ratings assigned in 7 PERs validated by IEG, 50 were confirmed (79 percent), 1 was raised (2 percent), and 8 were lowered (13 percent).

So far, IEG has assessed two of seven PERs as "good practice." This is a 29 percent rate and is about equal to IFC's percentage of best practice XPSRs—both at the beginning of its program and in 2011.

ANALYSIS

Self-evaluation is an instrument to extract lessons and identify risks and shortcomings in MIGA's underwriting. The Economics and Policy Group, which is overseeing MIGA's operational strategies, has undertaken some analysis based on the self-evaluations, including some that IEG has validated. The department analyzed the relationship between success rates and their drivers to specify the nature of MIGA's value added in projects. The analysis found that MIGA's added value resides more in deterring adverse country risk events than in improving financing terms or project structuring. MIGA has also started to synthesize lessons from project self-evaluations, including sponsors' experience, the importance of E&S monitoring and timely follow-up, and the critical role of the regulatory regime in infrastructure projects.

CORPORATE-LEVEL MONITORING AND EVALUATION

MIGA has modestly improved its ability to track implementation of its strategy. Based on its FY09–11 corporate strategy, MIGA adopted five key performance indicators in 2009: (1) volume of guarantee issues, (2) number of projects supported, (3) guarantees in IDA countries, (4) MIGA's return on operating capital, and (5) the ratio of administrative expense to net premium income ratio. These indicators align with four corporate priorities (projects in IDA countries, conflict-affected environments, complex infrastructure projects, and South-South investments).

Notes

1. These reports contained details about IFC's investments and provided an instrument for departmental portfolio reviews and checking project data and other areas not reviewed regularly by the portfolio staff (for example, technical/financial completion and technical assistance provided). Information in the PSR was mainly drawn from other IFC databases, and only about 10 percent was new. Because of this duplication, the PSR was discontinued at the end of December 2011 and integrated into the CRR by expanding its template to incorporate the annual data that were in the PSR.

2. CDC Group plc. had external assurance conducted by an audit firm in 2010 on its processes to implement its Investment Code but not on its development impact. CDC is also moving toward introduction of a system that is a scaled-down version of DOTS.

3. Decision documents in the screening and appraisal stages are Early Review, Summary of Proposed Investment, Pre-Appraisal/Appraisal, Investment Review Meeting, and Board Approval.

4. The process comprises (1) obtaining information from clients on E&S compliance according to the legal agreements; (2) reviewing the documents and making judgments on status; (3) assigning E&S risk ratings; and (4) if needed, conducting site visits or other follow-ups. The heart of the supervision is review of clients' Annual Monitoring Reports and Environmental and Social Action Plan reports. In 2006, IFC started using the Environmental and Social Risk Rating system to identify, rate, and monitor performance indicators, with the goal of minimizing the E&S footprint. This measures a project's E&S risk, using a proprietary model. IFC also makes selective site visits to high-risk projects.

5. In the portfolio sample of 90 projects, 12 projects were Global Trade Finance Facility projects, which do not use DOTS for tracking results and no data are entered in the system. Moreover, additionalities are not assessed for investments through risk management products and right issues.

6. CDI sends out a portfolio review template to have consistency among the data received. Teams doing the portfolio review are given guideline documents that lay down rules and guidelines for things such as acceptable reasons for assigning a too early to judge rating. In this process, the department does not have overwriting authority and thus has to reach an understanding with the relevant regional/industry team to decide on the missing gaps and how to fill them.

7. Big contributors are companies that represent at least 10 percent of the aggregated value for an indicator by industry and regional department. Big variations refer to projects where values on indicators change significantly (reduce by more than

30 percent or increase by more than 70 percent) in year-to-year value and have an absolute value increase of more than 0.5 percent of IFC's total aggregated indicator corresponding to it.

8. This is monitored by the Completion Status Report. This is a systematic report that refers to a weekly status update on the completion status of the mandatory indicators and DOTS ratings for all selected investments. There are three states for each investment: completed (all necessary values have been filled), in progress, and not started. Coverage for this report is limited to mandatory indicators by sector and also by region.

9. The first two years of assurance were conducted by Corporate Citizenship. Ernst and Young has handled this work for the past four years.

10. The review was in accordance with the International Standards for Assurance Engagements 3000, that is, International Standard on Assurance Engagements from International Federation of Accountants. The external assurance's independence is defined by the Federation's professional code of ethics (IFC 2012).

11. IEG often uses information that came after the XPSR finalization in its validation exercises, and that could partly contribute to the differences in project outlook between staff and IEG's team.

12. Currently, Advisory Services involves nearly 1,200 IFC staff, about 80 percent of whom are in field offices. In FY12, Advisory Services program spending totaled nearly $200 million. There has been increased business in Africa and South Asia, which now account for 43 percent of overall advisory spending. This service is funded by clients, donors, IFC's retained earnings, and other IFC sources.

13. The staff survey found that 86 percent of staff sought input from M&E officers when preparing a project's development outcome statements. This is a higher rate than regional business line leaders (67 percent of staff consulted them) or global business practice specialists (60 percent). All M&E officers provided input on project objectives and gave advice on indicators. A significant number (80 percent) also advised on project design (for example, for achieving better development impact). However, fewer than half of M&E officers (40 percent) provided lessons learned from prior projects, inputs on strategic fit, or additionality.

14. Initially 100 percent of eligible PCRs, then an annual sample of 70–80 percent and now 51 percent sample on three-year rolling average, starting in 2012.

15. Collection of baseline data has been a focus in the new governance policy (starting in FY11) and requires staff to define their pre-implementation budgets and set aside necessary funds for scoping and baseline data collection. At the Concept Note stage, the project team proposes a budget for pre-implementation activities, such as scoping, baseline data collection and analysis, feasibility analysis, and so forth. The budget for such activities should not exceed $100,000 or 10 percent of the overall project budget, whichever is lower.

16. The network also helped creating standard job titles, competencies framework, and terms of reference for M&E specialists in IFC to facilitate closer communication within the network and professionalization of the Results Measurement career stream within IFC.

17. IEG validated 100 percent of PCRs prepared for IFC Advisory Services during FY08-09. Beginning in FY10, IEG moved to a sampling approach, selecting a stratified (by business line) random sample from the population of PCRs (51 percent sampling rate three year rolling average). The sampling rate is set at a level sufficient to make inferences about success rates in the population at the 95 percent confidence interval with a sampling error of +/–5 percent or less. Among the sampling criteria used is the indicative development effectiveness self rating from the PCR. IEG excludes from its population PCRs prepared for non-client facing and knowledge products.

18. IEG's criteria for rating quality dimensions as "some extent" is based on evaluators' findings of important shortfalls, akin to Partly Unsatisfactory.

19. IEG rated TSTJ where insufficient achievement in outcomes made it impossible to assign a development effectiveness rating by completion, but where there was evidence of clear momentum and a likelihood that with a bit more time results may emerge.

20. IEG rated development effectiveness in cases where outcomes achievements were assessed, even in instances where it was too soon to judge impacts. However, if outcomes were assigned TSTJ or CV, IEG for the most part also assigned TSTJ and CV for development effectiveness. In this sense, outcome achievement was likely the most important dimension in considering the development effectiveness rating, while strategic relevance, efficiency, and outputs and impacts also played a role in determining the overall development effectiveness rating.

21. This refers to projects for which impacts were not deemed "not applicable" by having met IFC's Impact Exclusion Criteria.

22. IEG's approach to assessing financial intermediaries' sustainability and impacts beyond the financial intermediaries on sub-borrowers and overall market development for Advisory Services projects in the PCRs reviewed is based largely on concepts derived from IFC's XPSR framework.

23. Among the mature projects, MIGA selects few for self-evaluation every year (up to eight) and IEG independently evaluates the remaining ones.

24. These are the same as IFC's disagreements. Three of four disagreements involved rating of additionality as a part of work quality rather than a separate dimension of performance, and one involved methodology of assessing the business success of loans to financial intermediaries.

25. This excludes financial sector projects for which no E&S work was needed beyond initial project screening.

References

Dalberg Global Development Advisors. 2010. *The Glowing Role of the Development Finance Institutions in International Development Policy.* Copenhagen.

DFID (Department for International Development—United Kingdom). 2011. *Multilateral Aid Review: Ensuring Maximum Value for Money for UK Aid through Multilateral Organizations.* March 2011.

ECG (Evaluation Cooperation Group). 2011. *Good Practice Standards for Evaluation of Private Sector Operations,* rev. ed. http://www.ecgnet.org/gps/.

Gordon, K. 2008. "Investment Guarantees and Political Risk Insurance: Institutions, Incentives and Development." *OECD Investment Policy Perspectives* 2008, 91–122. Paris: OECD.

IEG (Independent Evaluation Group). 2008. *Biennial Report on Operations Evaluation: IFC's Results Measurement for Better Results.* Washington, DC: World Bank.

——. 2012. *World Bank Group Impact Evaluations: Relevance and Effectiveness.* Washington, DC: World Bank.

——. 2013. *Results and Performance of the World Bank Group: 2012.* Washington, DC: World Bank.

IFC (International Finance Corporation). 2012. *Annual Report.* Washington, DC: World Bank.

Nathan Associates, Inc. 2011. *Literature Review of Development Return to DFI's Investment in Private Enterprises.* London.

Chapter 3

Use and Influence of Monitoring and
Evaluation in IFC and MIGA

- M&E is providing lessons that can help management and staff select and structure projects.
- In IFC Investment and Advisory Services, the monitoring system effectively detected problems during implementation, and a majority of problems have been adequately addressed.
- IFC extensively uses its development outcome ratings in formulating strategies and in publicly reporting its results.
- Integrating Investment Services and Advisory Services has been a frequent strategic component, but IFC has separate M&E systems for these services, with little overarching use of information to illustrate development effects of joint activities.
- Individual learning from self-evaluation is taking place in MIGA.

This chapter examines the extent to which M&E information supports evidence-based decision making and learning in the design and implementation of projects, programs, and strategies. It is line with evaluative question 2 (see chapter 1). The analysis is segmented along instruments and stages, but M&E systems are part of a feedback process that enables continuous adjustments to improve results.

Use of Monitoring and Evaluation in IFC Projects

This evaluation comes at a time of growing focus on development results, in particular developing a shared understanding of what these are, strengthening the results measurement system, and improving the feedback into strategies and operations (IFC 2011). In the past, development objectives were stated in general terms; with the introduction of IDGs, IFC is defining and standardizing development indicators to assess progress against targets. A critical part of the reform of the M&E system is the integration of various tracking mechanisms into a results management system.

AT ENTRY

Investment Projects

XPSRs are part of a systematic process for generating lessons from mature investment projects to improve the selection and structure of new projects. IFC has not produced a significant number of project impact or program evaluations for investment projects, and XPSRs are the main source of lessons. IFC's Project Data Sheet-Early Review document had a section to describe relevant lessons from past projects. Investment officers use multiple sources to find the lessons—XPSRs, IFC databases, and advice from sector specialists. It is not possible to pinpoint the source of each lesson, but most lessons have been part of the outputs of XPSRs (see box 3.1).

IFC staff are increasingly decentralized, making identifying relevant sector- and country-related lessons or expertise more challenging. A survey of IFC investment officers found that the most frequent source of expertise at the early review and appraisal stage is IFC industry specialists. The E-LRN database contains every lesson written by IFC staff in XPSRs since 1996. There are about 3,000 lessons covering more than 100 countries and 20 primary sectors. E-LRN allows staff to search lessons based on many criteria, including environmental category, funding instrument, and theme. Staff can rate and comment on the lessons to help identify the more useful lessons and to share expertise.

Source: IEG.

In a sample[1] of investment projects evaluated by IEG during FY08–11, 85 percent articulated lessons from previous projects in the Project Data Sheet-Early Review document, typically three to five lessons from various sources. The lessons serve as a basis for defining the areas of focus during appraisal, but neither the Project Data Sheet-Early Review document nor the Investment Review Memorandum articulates how the lessons were incorporated in project structuring. The document was recently revised (now called "Project Data Sheet – Concept"), eliminating the lessons learned section; this may reduce the use of the lessons in decision making.

A review of unsuccessful projects showed that some lessons were not cited in the early review process. Of the projects that IEG evaluated FY08–11, 54 percent were rated mostly unsuccessful or worse. In 80 percent of the unsuccessful[2] projects, low quality at entry was a main factor leading to poor development outcomes. A review of the unsuccessful projects with low quality at entry showed that in about 40 percent of the cases, lessons relating to the factors responsible for poor performance were not identified at entry, though they should have been well known from previous projects (see table 3.1). A major challenge is identifying the lessons appropriate for a particular context; there is a tendency to copy lessons

Table 3.1 | Unidentified Lessons in Unsuccessful Projects

Lesson area	Number
Sponsor quality	5
Accompanying technical assistance	3
Corporate governance	3
Environmental and social	3
Political uncertainty	2
Regulatory issues	1
South-South investment	1
Venture funds	1

Source: IFC.

from similar projects. The recently re-introduced E-LRN database should make it easier to find the salient lessons.

In about 60 percent of unsuccessful projects with poor quality at entry, the lessons in the Project Data Sheet-Early Review documents were appropriate and relevant. However, during screening, appraisal, and structuring (SAS) the lessons were not integrated into the project design (see box 3.2). There is scope for improving SAS, and both Advisory Services and E&S have used mechanisms to improve quality at entry (see discussion below).

Box 3.2	Incorporating Lessons in Agribusiness Projects

An IEG evaluation in the early 2000s found that the performance of IFC's agribusiness had been unsatisfactory. However, its performance since the turn of the millennium has steadily improved. By 2010, it had become one of the higher-performing sectors.

IEG reviewed the 14 agribusiness XPSRs between 2000 and 2010 to determine the extent to which lessons translated into better projects and outcomes. There were eight in 2000–04 (Group 1) and six in 2005–10 (Group 2). The development outcome success rate for Group 1 is 50 percent; for Group 2, it is 80 percent. The 14 XPSRs produced 34 lessons, 23 (68 percent) from Group 1 and 11 (32 percent) from Group 2. Most lessons (74 percent) are about the project appraisal due diligence process. The rest are about monitoring.

This review revealed two examples of evaluation findings influencing the appraisal process. First, lessons in the Group 2 projects were noticeably different from those in Group 1. This suggests that the quality concerns at project entry (the dimension that featured dominantly in Group 1 projects) had been overcome, possibly through learning from past mistakes. This is in line with improved XPSR ratings for screening, appraisal, and structuring: Group 1 projects had 38 percent satisfactory or better ratings, but Group 2 had 83 percent (five of six).

Second, the Group 2 projects with high-quality work each reflected lessons from Group 1 projects:

- Project 1: The appraisal report referenced: strengthening the management team, developing a "Plan B" to mitigate potential technical harvest failure; and scaling up the operation commensurate with management capacity.

- Project 2: The project discussion explicitly addressed unusual weather conditions in the risk discussion.

- Project 3: One document shows adoption of lessons on using a highly professional team to manage a family company.

- Project 4: A document highlighted the importance of commodity price volatility, which has implications in delaying the project implementation.

- Project 5: A document pointed out that the project's profitability was highly dependent on commodity price variations. It also pointed out the "key-man risk" of unclear leadership succession planning.

It is difficult to establish concrete linkages between lessons in the appraisal documents and lessons adopted. There was an emphasis on agribusiness as a strategic sector, and that may also contribute to project improvements.

Source: IEG.

The early review and appraisal processes for E&S have guidelines and lessons for investment officers on due diligence and how to work with E&S specialists. The Environmental and Social Review Process manual recommends practices that complement specialists' professional judgment and expertise. There are three principles of quality assurance: (1) fit for purpose—the product should be suitable for the purpose; (2) right the first time—mistakes should be eliminated; and (3) continuous improvement. Lessons from past projects are embodied in this quality assurance process, and high-risk projects are subject to greater scrutiny.

These practices and changes in E&S resources have been reflected in IEG's ratings for IFC's E&S appraisal quality, including evaluation of IFC's site visit or desk review for identifying E&S risks and requirements, adequacy of Environmental Impact Assessment and Environmental and Social Action Plan, screening to A, B, C or FI category, preparing and disclosing ESRD, and transferring the E&S and reporting requirements to loan covenants and other legal documents. IFC's E&S appraisal has been strong for real-sector (nonfinancial intermediary) projects, with constant above 90 percent success rate after 2005, as shown in figure 3.1. The deterioration of appraisal quality for FI projects evaluated 2004–09 is explained by the five-year lag between appraisal and evaluation; the number of appraised FI projects increased 37 percent between 1999 and 2004, and their share of environmental categories (A, B, and FI) increased from 28 percent to 41 percent. During that period, there were only one or two E&S specialists in IFC's Environmental, Social and Governance Department to both appraise and supervise the increasing number of financial intermediary projects. Since 2006, staff for the financial intermediary sector has increased to eight E&S specialists and eight consultants. IEG believes that accounts for the reversal of declining E&S appraisal work quality; in 2011 the success rate of IFC's appraisal quality for FI projects was 84 percent.

These practices and institutional mechanisms contributed to IEG's rating of 87 percent satisfactory or better in 2011 for overall work quality at appraisal of projects' E&S dimension. Figure 3.1 shows the trend in work quality at appraisal for E&S. The Environmental and Social Department has been responsive to evaluation outcomes, as when work quality at appraisal for financial institution projects fell from 92 percent in 2008 evaluations to 72 percent in 2009. This led to improvements in the appraisal process, resulting in a reversal of the decline and a satisfactory or better rating of 84 percent in 2011.

The early review process explicitly considers a project's development impacts and its contribution to development goals. The revised template discusses strategic context, additionality, and development impacts ahead of financial and business aspects. The template considers strategic relevance, identification and measurement of development outcomes, articulation of how the project leads to higher-order outcomes, and the risks to PSD or poverty-related outcomes. However, lessons in the Project Data Sheet-Early Review documents relate mainly to project business success and compliance with E&S standards. In addition, strategic relevance of the project and sustainability of outcomes are not part of the project evaluation framework; hence, lessons on these aspects do not appear in XPSRs. There is a

| **Figure 3.1** | Trends in IFC's E&S Appraisal Work Quality Evaluated 2004–11 |

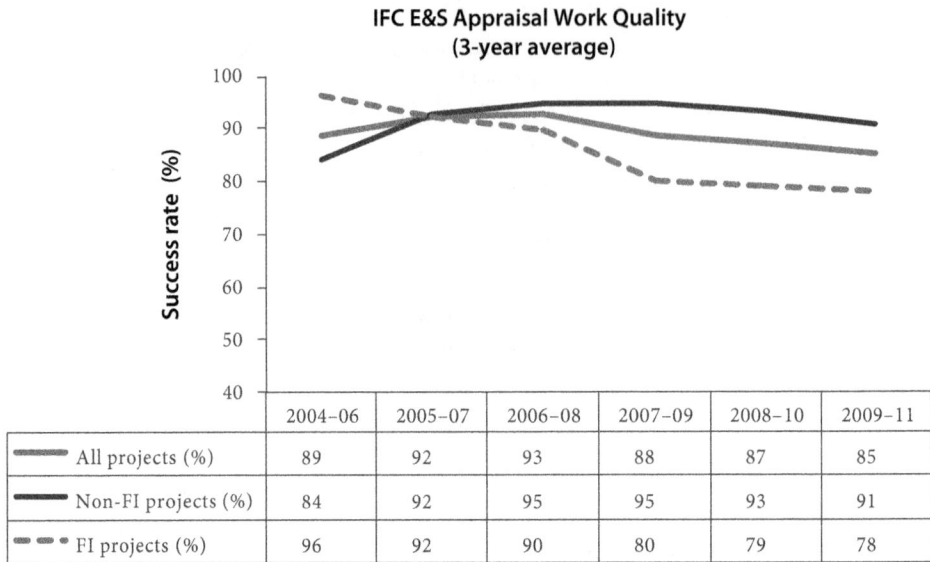

**IFC E&S Appraisal Work Quality
(3-year average)**

	2004–06	2005–07	2006–08	2007–09	2008–10	2009–11
All projects (%)	89	92	93	88	87	85
Non-FI projects (%)	84	92	95	95	93	91
FI projects (%)	96	92	90	80	79	78

Source: IEG.

Note: Years are evaluation year, judging appraisal work of five years before maturity. E&S = environmental and social; FI = financial intermediary.

growing body of experience on how to increase development impacts—for example, programmatic approaches, integration of Advisory Services and investments, or sequencing of investment projects with reforms—which is not incorporated in the lessons learned section.

Advisory Services

There is a wealth of lessons from PCRs and external thematic evaluations (including impact evaluations). PCR authors are prompted to provide lessons in 10 areas, including project design, implementation, development results, and client commitment. The segmentation would help task managers find lessons for distinct aspects of project design. A survey of Advisory Services staff involved with project preparation found that about 75 percent used PCRs as inputs. Advisory Services also makes extensive use of impact evaluations; these typically contain relevant lessons, especially where activities are being scaled up or replicated (IEG 2012). With regard to the impact evaluations, some provided new information or new insights and IFC distributed through business lines and through learning events, but some impact evaluation did not have any new lessons and had limited applicability to operational work.

IFC's SmartLessons[3] is cataloging lessons, mainly from the Advisory Services operations. SmartLessons contains 647 lessons, but 41 percent of Advisory Services staff (at project preparation) and 60 percent of Advisory Services results measurement officers said they never used them.

In FY08, the PDS document was revised to include a section that identifies appropriate lessons and describes how they have been applied to the project's design. In a sample[4] of projects that used the revised document, about 80 percent of the lessons learned sections had been filled. About 15 percent answered "not applicable"—mainly pilot projects or new products. Another five percent left the section blank. With the modification, there is more systematic use of the lessons from evaluations. As more projects use this template, it will be possible to compare projects with and without the explicit use of evaluation lessons.

IFC work quality (project design and implementation) has been a major contributor to poor results. IEG found that 72 percent of unsuccessful projects got low ratings because of poor implementation and design (IEG 2013). Lack of proper indicators and baseline data, unclear objectives, and unrealistic outputs and outcomes contributed to poor design. To improve designs, M&E specialists advise on all new Advisory Services projects to help articulate the development case, define objectives, and develop the M&E system, including indicators. Also, CDI has started to work with regions to improve project design. Ninety-six percent of survey respondents report that they have sought input from M&E specialists in defining project objectives.

MONITORING PROJECT IMPLEMENTATION

Investment Projects

There has been sustained high-quality supervision. IEG rated 83 percent of the projects as satisfactory or better for supervision, compared with 59 percent for screening, appraisal, and structuring. Interaction with clients was the main mechanism to validate information to track performance—90 percent of survey respondents contacted clients to clarify nonfinancial information. In a sample of XPSRs during FY08–11, half identified supervision issues, of which 90 percent were in PSRs. This is indicative of the effectiveness of the monitoring system in revealing implementation issues. Sixty-three percent of the issues in the PSRs were addressed fully during supervision; most of the 37 percent where supervision action was incomplete or delayed were issues related to environmental reporting.

DOTS is the main instrument for monitoring development outcomes, and there have been continuous efforts to improve data. Based on interviews with staff, DOTS is not a major source of information to adjust projects during supervision: less than 10 percent use M&E[5] information to make adjustments during supervision. There are two explanations. First, staff use other monitoring tools—such as the CRR and Environmental and Social Risk Rating systems—for issues relating to project business success and E&S effects. In addition, the economic sustainability rating is closely linked to project business success. Second, staff have limited scope to make adjustments where PSD outcomes are lagging.

IFC's E&S supervision is based on reviewing clients' Annual Monitoring Reports and visiting project sites. For nonfinancial intermediary projects, IFC requires that the client comply with at-appraisal E&S requirements that include IFC's Safeguard Policies (pre-2006) or IFC Performance Standards (post-2006), Environmental, Health and Safety Guidelines, the E&S Action Plan, and other project-specific E&S requirements. For financial intermediary projects, IFC requires that the client implement a Social and Environmental Management System and that subprojects comply with host country laws, exclusion list, and performance standards, depending on portfolio risks. IFC's supervision of nonfinancial intermediary projects has been satisfactory or better in about 80 percent of the projects since 2006, but the understaffed financial intermediary sector supervision before 2006 has resulted in below satisfactory ratings in nearly half of the projects (figure 3.2). This situation has been gradually corrected with increasing staff resources, and with 16 E&S specialists working in the financial intermediary sector in 2011, the supervision quality of financial intermediary projects is now about at the same level as for nonfinancial intermediary projects.

Advisory Projects

PSRs are the principal instrument for monitoring project implementation. About 95 percent of survey respondents have used PSRs to make adjustments during supervision, with 60 percent of them using it all the time. An IEG review of FY08–10 PCRs showed that 88 percent of the supervision issues in PCRs were captured in the PSRs, indicating that supervision has taken into account issues that affect outputs and outcomes. Similarly, IEG found in a sample of Advisory Services PSRs that poor supervision was a critical

| Figure 3.2 | Trends in IFC's E&S Supervision Work Quality Evaluated 2004–11 |

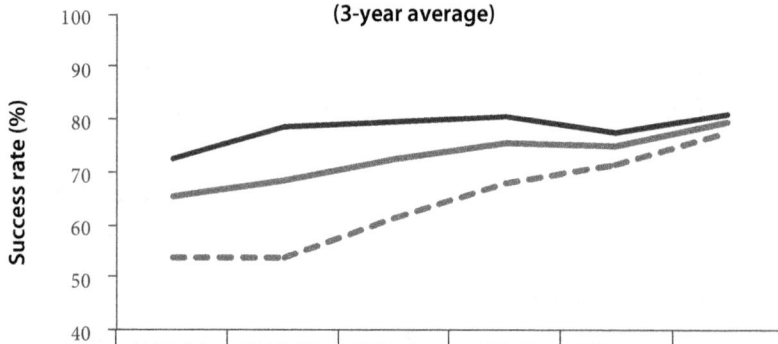

IFC E&S Supervision Work Quality (3-year average)

	2004–06	2005–07	2006–08	2007–09	2008–10	2009–11
All projects (%)	65	68	72	75	75	80
Non-FI projects (%)	72	79	80	81	77	81
FI projects (%)	54	53	61	68	72	78

Source: IEG.
Note: E&S = environmental and social; FI = financial intermediary.

factor in 25 percent of the projects rated mostly unsuccessful or worse for development effectiveness. PSRs have been relatively successful in identifying and monitoring implementation issues, and about 70 percent of the problems had been adequately addressed.

Integrating Development Results into Staff Incentive Structures in IFC

IFC is integrating a development focus into staff incentives. IFC uses DOTS ratings as the indicator for project development performance in the Corporate Scorecard. As an incentive, it introduced Department Scorecard Awards in FY02 to reward staff for contributing to scorecard objectives. The program was expanded to the entire Corporation in FY10 as the Corporate Scorecard Award and is based on development impacts (measured by projects' development results ratings), client satisfaction, profitability, productivity, and growth.

The Long-Term Performance Awards Program for investment staff began in 2004 to recognize development and financial results of projects that staff brought into the portfolio five to eight years earlier. Every year, IFC compares the development outcome of each investment staff member's "portfolio" based on IEG-validated XPSR or DOTS ratings or proxies based on credit risk ratings. Staff that score above average are then compared in terms of financial returns to IFC. This system, based on development outcomes, is unique among MDBs.

The IDGs will become part of the Scorecard, and directors' and managers' performances are assessed on new projects' contributions to the IDGs. This is balanced with other Scorecard elements, such as projects in IDA countries, to reduce perverse incentives. IDGs are not used directly in annual staff performance ratings.

Similarly, for Advisory Services, development effectiveness ratings are part of directors' and managers' performance assessment indicators, and development effectiveness success rate targets typically cascade down to all operational staff performance objectives. This enhances their responsiveness to results.

Increasing the use of results indicators is a double-edged sword. It moves IFC in the right direction and focuses attention on the development mission, but it creates incentives for upward-biased self-evaluation ratings and information. The increasing gaps between XPSR self-ratings and IEG's independent ratings show that there is a growing tendency to self-rate positively.

USE OF MONITORING AND EVALUATION IN IFC STRATEGIES

Strategy Development

IFC's strategies provide guidance on project choices to increase development impact. Regional, industry cluster, and Advisory Services strategies identify focus areas over a three-year horizon. The strategies are reviewed and updated every year, typically with management discussions in December or January of the preceding fiscal year. The Strategy Department provides guidelines on what should be included in the strategies and helps the departments develop them.[6]

The annual strategy process is the principal forum of strategic choice. With IFC's greater focus on development impact,[7] the role of CDI has gained importance. During its strategy session in November 2010, the department discussed how to bring evidence and lessons of development effectiveness into strategy, operations, and new business decision making. It provides data and participates in departmental and regional strategy discussions, as well as the senior management retreat.

For FY13–15, the Strategy Department flagged the decline in development results in IDA countries[8] and requested that departments consider what this would mean for strategy and what actions could reverse the trend. The departments were also asked to recommend which issues to address in prospective evaluations, specifically with respect to measuring and improving development impacts. IFC recognizes knowledge gaps, such as on poverty impact of IFC activities, and part of the CDI's support is to help departments plan to reduce the gaps.

Development results ratings for Investment Services and Advisory Services are widely used, but to varying degrees, in strategy formulation. Manufacturing, Agribusiness and Services (MAS) used a loan performance framework consisting of historical DOTS ratings and effective loan spreads to compare performance among sectors. The framework helped prioritize and classify sectors into strategic, core, noncore, and not supported, with anticipated improvements in future DOTS ratings.[9] In the case of Financial Markets and the Eastern and Southern Europe and Central Asia Region, the decline in DOTS performance was seen as temporary, caused by the financial crisis, and did not lead to a strategic shift. In the Africa and the Middle East and North Africa Regions, declining DOTS ratings were recognized in the FY13–15 strategies. They did not result in strategic course corrections but will be addressed through better project selection.

Gap analysis using the "reach indicators" (the number of people served by IFC's clients) has been featured in strategy formulation. In Financial Markets, the strategy focused on improving access for 2.5 billion people and 300 million MSMEs without access to financial services in emerging markets. The strategic implication was an increased focus on Asia and Africa, which accounted for about 75 percent of the financial access gap. In South Asia, gaps in access to various services by people at the base of the pyramid—water, electricity, telecom, and financial services—were measured and used to underpin the economic inclusion pillar of the South Asia strategy and identify the indicators to measure IFC contribution to reducing gaps. Latin America and the Caribbean used the same gap analysis to developing a strategy to reach the bottom of the pyramid (see table 3.2). The same measure was used to analyze contribution to climate change—the Asia strategy targets a one percent reduction in greenhouse gas emissions in the region by 2014 as a result of IFC activities.

The increased focus on poverty has led to a growth/inclusiveness strategic framework. CDI found that the bulk of the portfolio promotes broad-based growth that indirectly benefits the poor, and that many current strategies have activities that promote inclusiveness, which directly benefits the poor. The development

Table 3.2	Gaps and Targets at Bottom of the Pyramid in Latin America and the Caribbean		
Sector	Gap	Current reach	Expected reach by 2013
Education	18 million students	1 million students	4 million students
Microcredit	29 million clients	4.2 million loans	8 million loans
Health	41 million patients	1.5 million patients	4 million patients
Housing	30 million homes	240,000 homes	480,000 homes
Source: IFC.			

of the Poverty Action Plan includes a review of how industry strategies could systematically target the poor and define the mix of growth and inclusiveness projects. Two strategies—for Financial Markets and the Europe, Middle East and North Africa Region—used the growth/inclusiveness framework to identify the distribution of current activities and to guide project selection. Still there is no common definition of poverty or poverty objectives, resulting in inconsistent tracking and evaluation of poverty results.[10]

Most strategies do not analyze the efficiency of strategic choices; exceptions are Financial Markets and Latin America and the Caribbean. The Financial Markets strategy used a framework that compared strategic options' development and financial returns. Reach indicators were used to measure development returns per dollar of cost and capital. Based on the framework and the relative importance of development and financial returns, the areas of focus would differ. In the Financial Markets framework, projects focusing on trade and equity would maximize the number of people served by IFC's clients in a capital-constrained environment. The Latin America and the Caribbean strategy used relative share of the region in the IFC portfolio and various reach indicators to show the efficiency with which it used capital for development.

Some strategies incorporate lessons from XPSRs and results from external evaluations. In the agribusiness sector, findings from project evaluations were major inputs to a new strategy. Advisory Services has been more systematic in using results from PCRs and external evaluations in strategies, such as in scaling up selected programs in microfinance and secured transactions. The ad hoc nature of external evaluations and the fragmentation of XPSR lessons have limited the use of evaluation results. There is a growing body of evaluative evidence—mainly at the project level—but it is not in a format that would be useful for strategy formulation. For example, a recent internal IEG review of the extractive industries cluster came up with strategic lessons, most of which were not in the XPSRs (see box 3.3).

Strategies include initiatives, programs or programmatic approaches, but M&E systems are project based. The programs are at multiple levels: global (for example, Supply Chain Integration), regional (Education for Employment in the Arab Youth), or country (Health in India Initiative). These do not have systematic arrangements for M&E that would provide useful lessons for future program design and strategy formulation, although external evaluators have reviewed some

Advisory Services programs. Impact evaluation results have been used in scaling up or replicating some Advisory Services programs and have been useful inputs to strategies. As part of the Country Assistance Strategy process, there is an M&E system for country programs. However, CASCRs lack useful lessons for program design, in part because they examine World Bank interventions extensively in all sectors, with IFC typically a peripheral factor in non-joint CASCRs.

Integrating Investment and Advisory Services has been a major component of strategies. Advisory Services has been used to unlock market potential, enabling entry of IFC investments and private investment—an example would be Advisory Services assisting a government to establish institutional arrangements for PPPs, with a subsequent IFC investment in a PPP. Parallel Advisory Services in areas such as investment climate and financial infrastructure can improve the development results from IFC investments (see box 3.4).

Advisory Services also provides direct assistance to IFC investment clients; in many cases technical assistance is integral to the design of investment projects to strengthen capacity and corporate governance. The Europe and Central Asia strategy used an integrated Investment Services/Advisory Services approach toward its climate change goals and support to the bottom of the pyramid. The East Asia and the Pacific strategy focused on the "one IFC" approach, with integrated country-level investment and advisory programs. In the infrastructure cluster, Advisory Services had a significant role in the strategy for reaching difficult and emerging sectors and for consolidating IFC client companies' licenses to operate. In Financial Markets and MAS, Advisory Services were used strategically to increase reach, for instance, through secured lending and programs that increase local purchases. The "one IFC" approach was rolled out in FY10 as a systematic approach across the corporation.

Monitoring Strategy Implementation

Strategies articulate main priorities or areas of focus and provide indicators to monitor progress against plans or targets. DOTS ratings are the main indicator

IEG recognized IFC's work on microfinance in Afghanistan as transformational in its Country Program Evaluation; an integrated Investment Services/Advisory Services approach was instrumental in achieving results. In 2003, IFC invested in the first commercial bank under the new banking laws—the First Microfinance Bank of Afghanistan. That bank was also the pioneer commercial microfinance institution; at that time, microfinance was dominated by donors and nongovernmental organizations.

The initial IFC investment was accompanied by a comprehensive Advisory Services project to build institutional capacity. A study of housing microfinance led to a new product by the bank that received technical assistance from Advisory Services. Another Advisory Services initiative helped the First Microfinance Bank of Afghanistan develop a strategy of outreach to female entrepreneurs, with positive results. The bank helped sustain microfinance lending during the financial crisis. In 2011, the First Microfinance Bank of Afghanistan accounted for almost half of the microfinance disbursements.

Source: IEG 2012.

for development outcomes, though these are not disaggregated according to strategic priorities or pillars. There is growing use of reach indicators, aggregated from the project-level results, to measure progress. Hence there is standardized measurement at project and strategy levels, although there are strategic priorities that do not have overarching reach or outcome indicators, such as competitive markets and competitiveness. Table 3.3 shows the regional priorities and reach indicators.

The relation of Investment and Advisory Services projects to strategic themes has been an important indicator. The shares of IDA countries, fragile and conflict-affected states, frontier regions in middle-income countries, and the base of the

Table 3.3   Reach or Outcome Indicators in Regional Strategies

Strategic pillar or focus	Reach or outcome indicators
Inclusive growth	People reached
Investment climate	Doing Business ranking and number of reforms
Competitiveness	(No single indicator to measure competitiveness)[a]
Global/Regional integration	South-South investment
Climate change	CO_2 emission avoided
MSME	Clients reached
Infrastructure	People reached
Agribusiness	Farmers reached

Source: IFC.

Note: MSME = micro, small, and medium-size enterprise.

[a] For competitiveness, indicators are specified based on country or regional contexts and IFC's focus. For example, energy efficiency, food safety, and corporate governance indicators were used to measure outcomes in the area of competitiveness in the Europe and Central Asia Region.

pyramid segment have been used to track poverty focus. Projects in priority sectors or themes (for example, agribusiness, climate change, and regional integration) are also monitored. Portfolio shares are reported annually and compared with targets and prior years. The indicators affect project choices and point to areas where performance is problematic. From a macro standpoint, achieving both the allocation targets and maintaining DOTS ratings is an indicator of successful implementation of strategies.

Weak use of indicators to measure a project's PSD effects beyond the company—for example, competitiveness and sectoral transformation—incorrectly estimates strategies' effectiveness in the PSD. More generally, the indicators count the reach of projects but do not account for strategies' higher-level goals.

Strategies have generally responded to lagging indicators. Slow progress toward reach indicators resulted in a re-evaluation of the Financial Markets strategy and adoption of new approaches. MAS tracks the gap between IFC-wide and cluster DOTS performance to determine whether its revised strategy is working. Financial infrastructure activities are being scaled up based on evaluations of earlier interventions. Improving the relevance and timeliness of development results indicators, including establishing an M&E system for programs, would give management a stronger basis for adjustments during strategy implementation.

Use of Monitoring and Evaluation in MIGA Guarantee Projects and Strategy

M&E of development results from MIGA guarantee projects is relatively new. Monitoring of E&S aspects began three years ago, with staff performing regular supervision and reporting. The DEIS is being rolled out, modeled after DOTS. Given the nature of MIGA's business relationship with its guarantee clients, it is unclear how DEIS will affect project implementation. Direct investments give IFC contractual leverage; in addition, IFC is able to use instruments such as membership in Boards and technical assistance through Advisory Services to address issues that arise.

MIGA's self-evaluation process has now been mainstreamed. A self-evaluation is performed by the senior operational staff, who are also required to prepare other new projects, so it is expected that evaluation lessons will be internalized and will influence future projects and the quality of underwriting. In a survey of MIGA staff involved with self-evaluation, more than 70 percent responded that it improved their understanding of development impacts. MIGA's underwriting guideline requires review of relevant, documented experiences from prior guarantee projects and staff and management discuss such lessons at the decision meetings.

Notes

1. This is the same sample of investment projects used in chapter 2.

2. Unsuccessful projects are defined as those rated Mostly Unsuccessful or worse.

3. SmartLessons is a World Bank Group awards program that enables development practitioners to share lessons learned in development operations. SmartLessons are short papers (two to four pages), written by professionals for professionals; they share first-hand, practical lessons that can be useful for colleagues working on similar projects/programs or facing similar issues. SmartLessons are also available in video format (three to six minutes) through which lessons learned are presented in a short and concise audiovisual style (http://smartlessons.ifc.org/smartlessons/page.html?page=1427)).

4. This is the same sample of Advisory Services projects used in chapter 2.

5. The survey lists the following as M&E tools: DOTS, Advisory Services PCRs, Advisory Services PSRs, XPSRs, SmartLessons, IEG evaluations of IFC or World Bank, evaluations of IFC projects by consultants/IFC department, and evaluation reports of other parties (such as other development banks).

6. The Strategy Department drafts the annual IFC Road Map covering the next three fiscal years using the strategies as inputs. Summaries of regional strategies are part of the Road Maps.

7. In its guidance memo to the management team, the Strategy Department identified as the overarching topic how IFC should focus its activities and organization to deliver greater development impact, which supports poverty reduction and sustainable and inclusive growth, while serving clients better and remaining financially sustainable.

8. The *Results and Performance of the World Bank Group 2012* (IEG 2013) also flagged this trend.

9. The *Results and Performance of the World Bank Group 2012* (IEG 2013) reported increased performance of MAS and identified a change in strategy as a significant contributing factor.

10. Management response to the IEG report on poverty (IEG 2011).

References

IEG (Independent Evaluation Group). 2011. *Assessing IFC's Poverty Focus and Results.* Washington, DC: World Bank.

———. 2012. *World Bank Group Impact Evaluations: Relevance and Effectiveness.* Washington, DC: World Bank.

———. 2013. *Results and Performance of the World Bank Group 2012.* Washington, DC: World Bank.

IFC (International Finance Corporation). 2011. *IFC Road Map FY12–14: Impact, Innovation, and Partnership.* Washington, DC: World Bank.

Chapter 4

Effectiveness and Efficiency of Monitoring and Evaluation Systems

- By applying lessons from M&E, IFC can address the high-risk characteristics of an investment project and achieve better results.

- Good project design and implementation qualities drive positive results of IFC Advisory Services projects.

- For IFC Advisory Services, the link between strong M&E systems and greater project development effectiveness was not uniform across the business lines.

- Use of M&E information in MIGA is increasing, though it is still limited because of the relatively new program and the small number of evaluated projects from which to draw lessons. But underwriting staff indicate a powerful learning effect from direct involvement in evaluation.

- IFC spends about $14 million per year for M&E. It is challenging to assess the efficiency of these expenses, but a cost-benefit analysis can provide useful insights to systematically assess the efficiency of M&E efforts. It is estimated that the financial benefit for IFC alone can justify the M&E expenditure.

- MIGA has a distinct challenge of developing its M&E system in a cost-effective way that also reflects its development mandate and operational practices.

M&E generates information to improve efficiency and operational effectiveness. This chapter explores whether M&E has actually led to better projects and development outcomes in IFC and MIGA to answer two evaluative questions:

- To the extent that M&E outputs have been used, has this translated into better development outcomes and project quality?

- To the extent that impacts on development outcomes and project quality can be ascertained, are these impacts commensurate with costs?

M&E systems are neither necessary nor sufficient for good development outcomes. They are one among many components and conditions that jointly determine outcomes and impacts. The goal here is modest—to look for evidence of whether M&E systems contribute to IFC's and MIGA's development results, that is, whether they make a difference (Mayne 2012 has an introduction to contribution analysis).

Effectiveness of Monitoring and Evaluation Systems in IFC and MIGA

In IFC's Investment and Advisory Services, M&E is expected to lead to better results through improved project designs, timely and appropriate interventions during implementation, and a stronger strategic focus.

For investment projects, XPSRs and IEG's evaluations have identified project risks and IFC's work quality as the principal results drivers. One contributor to work quality is SAS, which evaluates IFC's project processing at entry looking back at the time of project maturity, applying hindsight reflection of at-entry work quality. This assesses whether IFC identified the most important risks that could reasonably have been foreseen and whether it effectively reduced or mitigated them. IFC cannot mitigate all risks, but the risk-reward profile should be acceptable. The other element of work quality is supervision and administration, which comprises IFC's activities from approval through closure, including monitoring projects' E&S performances.

IFC investment operations are inherently risky. By applying knowledge and experience, IFC can avoid, reduce, or mitigate these risks. One source of knowledge is lessons from the past. For example, sponsor risks are based on weak sponsor experience, commitment, financial capacity, or reputation. At appraisal, IFC has to determine whether it can work with the sponsor. There are 513 lessons in the XPSR lessons archives (E-LRN) related to sponsors' experience, due diligence, and aligning incentives through covenants, security, or other conditions. The market risk relates to businesses' competitiveness, and the appraisal process assesses a firm's likely profitability under market conditions, dynamics, and sensitivities to alternative parameters. E-LRN has 455 lessons about market risk assessment, and they offer advice on using industry benchmarks, conducting sensitivity analyses, and acceptable leverage ratios for different industries. Project type is the third type of risk. Specifically, greenfield projects share the specific risks of business start-ups, and lessons point to measures to assess, reduce, or mitigate these risks.

Based on evaluation of 10 projects appraised under the performance standards framework in the XPSR 2011 sample, IEG concludes that the performance standards provide a much better and wider set of indicators to identify, apprise and monitor the E&S risks, especially for the nonfinancial institutions projects compared with the previous safeguard policy framework. The online ESRD has been diligently used to record and rate the individual themes under the eight performance standards at appraisal, but the use of the ESRD system for monitoring has been inadequate. In most cases the information available from clients' Annual Monitoring Reports and their reviews and E&S specialists' site visits has not been adequately transferred to ESRD supervision documents. This deficiency seriously limits the efficiency of the ESRD system for monitoring and ex post evaluation of E&S effects of IFC projects. The ESRD also lacks important theme indicators on air emissions, effluents, and waste management that constitute key E&S risks in most projects in process and manufacturing industry sectors.

IEG has found that in unsuccessful projects with weak appraisals, there was often a failure to acknowledge the lessons from E-LRN or other sources that were associated with the weak appraisal (see chapter 3). Among these projects, 42 percent did not describe relevant lessons in the appraisal documents. The other 58 percent had lessons documented, but they were not acted on. The consequences of not recognizing the lessons are that project risks were greater than they could have been and that the prospects of project success were diminished. Similarly, the case study of agribusiness projects (box 3.2) illustrates that finding and acting on lessons could be associated with better appraisals and development outcomes. By applying relevant lessons during screening, appraisal, and structuring, IFC can finance higher-risk projects without sacrificing its financial or development results, because the lessons suggest ways to reduce or mitigate the risks.

Moreover, there is a correlation between identification of relevant lessons and overall SAS work quality. The Project Data Sheet–Early Review had a "Lessons Learned" section to describe the salient lessons. This evaluation found in a sample of XPSRs that for projects with no documented lessons or superficial treatment of lessons, the SAS work is often rated less than satisfactory.[1] The sources of lessons vary; some credit M&E systems (such as E-LRN or XPSR lessons), but most are cited as IFC's experience or experiences in the relevant industry.

Another way to examine this is to estimate a regression in which XPSR's SAS work quality is a proxy for learning from experience with past projects—based on the above-identified correlation between lessons learned and SAS quality. The dependent variable is development outcome success, and the independent variables include the following:

- Sponsor risk (experience, financial capacity, commitment, and reputation of sponsor): 1 = high risk , 0 = low risk

- Market risk (business competitiveness in the market and distortion in the market): 1 = high risk, 0 = low risk

- Project type risk (greenfield start-up project versus expansion project): 1 = greenfield, 0 = expansion

- Changes in country business climate (changes in country risk indicators between approval and evaluation (that is, five years) score differences between evaluation and approval years.

- SAS work quality of XPSR: 1 = high (satisfactory and above), 0 = low

- Sponsor risk with high SAS work quality (high sponsor risk and high SAS work quality): 1 = high risk sponsor with high SAS work quality rating, 0 = else

- Market risk with high SAS work quality (high market risk and high SAS work quality): 1 = high risk market with high SAS work quality rating, 0 = else

- Project type risk with high SAS work quality (high project type risk and high SAS work quality): 1 = greenfield project with high SAS work quality rating, 0 = else

- Supervision work quality (XPSR rating of supervision and administration): 1 = high (satisfactory and above), 0 = low

- IFC role and contribution (XPSR ratings of IFC role and contribution): 1 = high (Satisfactory and above), 0 = low.

This equation was estimated using the 584 XPSRs in IEG's database, with the results summarized in table 4.1.

Table 4.1	Regression Results for Determinants of Development Outcome Success of IFC Investment Projects			
		(1)	(2)	(3)
Equation	Variables	Development outcome	Development outcome	Development outcome
Development outcome	Sponsor risk	−0.573***	−0.363***	−0.661***
		(0.114)	(0.140)	(0.207)
	Market risk	−0.457***	−0.439***	−0.141
		(0.120)	(0.146)	(0.221)
	Change in country risk	0.0237***	0.0134**	0.0150**
		(0.00504)	(0.00618)	(0.00628)
	Project type risk	−0.0446	−0.178	−0.456**
		(0.112)	(0.136)	(0.213)
	SAS work quality		0.889***	0.860***
			(0.140)	(0.277)
	Sponsor risk with high SAS work quality			0.552*
				(0.285)
	Market risk with high SAS work quality			−0.540*
				(0.300)
	Project type risk with high SAS work quality			0.458
				(0.280)
	Supervision and administration work quality		0.779***	0.783***
			(0.154)	(0.156)
	IFC roles and contribution work quality		1.423***	1.437***
			(0.186)	(0.190)
	Constant	0.757***	-1.388***	-1.384***
		(0.113)	(0.218)	(0.259)
	Observations	592	584	584

Source: IEG.
Note: Standard errors in parentheses; *** $p<0.01$, ** $p<0.05$, * $p<0.1$. SAS = screening, appraisal, and structuring stage.

The regression suggests that IFC work quality is the principal determinant of development outcome. In particular, front-end work quality (SAS) that reflects leaning and lessons—of experiences matters most. The interaction regression result (column 3) also suggests that high-quality SAS work mitigate high sponsor risk and leads to high development outcome. In contrast, high-quality SAS work quality is not sufficient to mitigate high market risk or lead to low development outcomes. High-quality SAS has no effect on project-type risk with regard to development outcome.

This finding can challenge a view that IFC should modify the success benchmark for high-risk environments (such as IDA countries) because of the inherent high risks. In fact, strong at-entry work, including adopting lessons up front and effective supervision, are potential factors to reduce or mitigate some of the project risks. As illustrated in the agribusiness project cases (box 3.2), early failures were sources of lessons, and their application to the subsequent projects might have contributed to better results.

IFC ADVISORY SERVICES

M&E influences an advisory project's outcome through two primary modes:

- The key ingredients for a successful outcome are clear objectives, baseline data, and relevant indicators. The M&E system provides a roadmap to achieve results. At the concept stage, it encourages a clear, precise program definition. Then it assists in implementing the design, raising the chances of success.

- The system facilitates corrective actions during supervision: M&E tracks progress by documenting results and design adjustments.

Forty-five percent of evaluated projects with development effectiveness ratings had high development outcomes and high M&E quality (based on whether the project has good logframe or uses relevant standard indicators). In contrast, about a quarter of projects have high-quality M&E but low development effectiveness. The systematic changes between M&E quality and development effectiveness suggest, through the method of concomitant variation, a correlation between the two.

Based on this, strong M&E systems can be associated with project effectiveness through better project design and execution. This hypothesis is based on a premise that the projects' development effectiveness is influenced by the quality of M&E through better design and stronger implementation. Good project design and implementation would improve projects' chances of success. IEG tested the hypothesis by using the evaluation database of Advisory Services projects to estimate the relationship between a project's development effectiveness ratings and preparation and its design and implementation. Furthermore, it is important to test the relationship between the project preparation and design and implementation of a project on the one hand, and the quality of appraisal and supervision on the other.

Unlike the investment project XPSRs, PCR do not contain assessment IFC's work quality. As the analysis of XPSRs indicated that the work quality is a strong determinant of projects' development outcome, IEG assessed work quality of 2008–10 PCRs for both project design and project implementation (see Appendix D for details of work quality criteria). Project design work quality rating was based on the categories such as appropriate mix of project activities, identification of committed counterparts, needs assessment, and tailoring of projects to local conditions. The rating for project implementation work quality was based on categories such as engagement with clients and stakeholders, work of consultants, and project management methods.

Based on the ratings assigned by IEG, 72 percent of low development effectiveness projects had poor designs caused by, for example, weak assessments of needs or markets, lack of clear objectives, unrealistic outputs and impacts, or inadequate activities to achieve objectives. Similarly, 61 percent of low development effectiveness projects had implementation shortcomings such as poor consultant work, weak client engagement and follow-up, ineffective coordination with donors, or insufficient staffing.

IEG tested the hypothesis that M&E quality influences outcomes through projects' design and implementation with a regression analysis. The dependent variable was the development effectiveness rating, and the independent variables were the quality of preparation and design, implementation, and M&E (in terms of use of appropriate logical model and indicators). There were 214 project evaluations (observations) to estimate the equation. In the multivariate regression (table 4.2), quality of design and quality of implementation were statistically significant, whereas the two indicators of quality of M&E were not.

One way to explain these regression results is that the project design and project implementation variables are correlated with M&E quality and are already reflected in M&E quality. In fact, M&E quality is an intrinsic part of project design and project management. The results therefore indicate that M&E quality has no independent effect on development effectiveness outside its effect on design and implementation. This is consistent with the hypothesis and is a symmetric result to the one obtained in the case of investment services.

Table 4.2	Regression Results for Determinants of Development Effectiveness Success of IFC Advisory Service Projects		
		(1)	(2)
Equation	Variables	Development effectiveness	Development effectiveness
Development effectiveness	Project design Work quality	1.325***	1.406***
		(0.230)	(0.245)
	Project implementation work quality	1.415***	1.465***
		(0.261)	(0.273)
	M&E quality (appropriate logframe)		−0.216
			(0.299)
	M&E quality (use of appropriate indicators)		−0.134
			(0.296)
	Constant	−1.620***	−1.457***
		(0.238)	(0.273)
	Observations	214	214

Source: IEG.
Note: Standard errors in parentheses; *** p<0.01, ** p<0.05, * p<0.1.

Learning Benefits from Self-Evaluation in MIGA

MIGA has a relatively brief history of self-evaluation and limited monitoring activities, and its use of M&E information is nascent. Nevertheless, three years of self-evaluations with a focus on staff learning has left initial impressions on MIGA staff.

The staff survey for this evaluation asked MIGA staff about learning from self-evaluations, and 67 percent responded that they had a better understanding of projects' development impacts and of MIGA's policies and procedures. Also, half the respondents answered that they had a better understanding of projects' risks to development outcomes and E&S risks. Separate interviews of MIGA staff revealed that participants found that evaluation was more demanding than underwriting, as it requires analysis of the financial and economic models and a critical reexamination of a project's life cycle. This imparted new insights about how to assess a project. For example, staff learned about results drivers for development outcomes, such as the role of investment climate and regulations in the power sector, as well as specific structuring experiences.

The survey also asked whether learning was applied to underwriting and business development. All answers were affirmative, and staff cited specific examples such as improving contract conditions or looking harder at project or contractual agreements in terms of risks to project revenues and cash flows. However, the major constraint is the small number of evaluations (IEG and self-evaluations) of MIGA projects, translated to small numbers of lessons available for MIGA staff. There are only a few lessons covering each sector, region, or theme. Lessons from self-evaluations are not integrated into the underwriting template. MIGA and IEG are seeking to open the lessons archive of IFC's XPSRs (E-LRN) so that MIGA staff can benefit from IFC experiences.

In addition to staff learning, self-evaluation has helped MIGA revised its Underwriting Guideline to improve the quality of MIGA's underwriting and make it consistent with self-evaluation guidelines. It—

- Encourages thoroughness and consistency among projects in the due diligence, risk analysis, and developmental and E&S impact assessments, and uniformity, quality, and focus of underwriting papers.
- Improves the relevance of due diligence, risk analysis, and development impact by dealing only with project-specific facts, risks, and development outcomes within the context of the host country's risk framework.

Under the guideline, MIGA is expected to produce a detailed, overall project risk assessment. The experiences of self-evaluation fed into the guideline, which is expected to increase the rigor and consistency of at-entry assessment.

Cost and Reach of Monitoring and Evaluation Systems

To the extent that impacts on development outcomes and project quality are realized, are they commensurate with costs? To illustrate the insights, a simplified cost effectiveness analysis was developed from cost information for each M&E instrument and compared against its use (table 4.3). This analysis cannot be extended to MIGA because of the early stage of integrating M&E into its business.

The costs for IFC Investment and Advisory Services were estimated using these assumptions:

- IFC investment XPSR—Based on IFC staff time sheet, average yearly staff-week over the past three years. Market reference salary of GF-level staff was used.

- DOTS—There is no budgetary tracking, and IEG estimated 10 percent of XPSR cost per project.

- CDI budget was $4.6 million, divided between Investment and Advisory Services.

- Advisory Services project M&E—because there is no budget breakdown, IEG used total project expenditure of FY12 and applied 3 percent (based on United Nations and USAID's "rule of thumb" number for M&E budget over project total expenditure). Regional M&E officers are based on staff salary estimates (four GF and four GG level staff).

- Thematic evaluation cost based on actual thematic evaluation spending in FY12 (data from CDI).

Based on these assumptions, IFC spends about $14 million per year for core M&E activities. This can be compared with the FY13 administrative budget of about $519 million, making the core M&E expenditure about 2.5 percent of the administrative budget.

Table 4.3	Estimated Cost of M&E Systems in IFC and MIGA		
	IFC Investment Services	IFC Advisory Services	MIGA
Project-level cost	Staff time for XPSR = $7,465 per XPSR ($522,000 per year) DOTS $0 (staff time not costed) to $747 (10% of XPSR). About $8,000 per project. 668 companies are featured in Annual Report ($498,996 total)	Total M&E cost estimated based on total program expenditure which is $197 million in FY12. Taking 3% of it is $5.9 million. There are 630 active projects = $9,400 per project on average per year, plus M&E officers in regions $0.9 million.	Self-evaluation $40,000 (including travel, staff time)
Thematic-level	Thematic = $0	Thematic $2.3million total/year	
Overheads	CDI $2.3 million	CDI $2.3 million	
Total	$7,465–10,965 per project XPSR+DOTS total $1.02 million plus DOTS overheads ($2.3 million)	$9,400 per project or $5.9 million total Plus Thematic, M&E officers and CDI overheads $5.5million	Assuming 10 self-evaluations per year
	$3.3 million/year	$11.4 million ear	$400,000/year

Source: IEG.
Note: CDI= Development Impact Department; DOTS = Development Outcome Tracking System; M&E = monitoring and evaluation; XPSR = Expanded Project Supervision Report.

In MIGA's self-evaluation, staff worked part time for self-evaluation for more than 34 weeks. Based on assumptions regarding team composition, staff grade, and travel costs, the average cost per evaluation is about $40,000, including travel costs (variable cost) of $25,000. The cost was estimated at $50,000 earlier but it came down as MIGA gained experiences in self-evaluation. This reflects the set-up cost of the self-evaluation system, MIGA's cost of obtaining and analyzing information because MIGA as an insurer does not routinely receive comparable operational and financial data from its clients and must gather data for each evaluation. MIGA also needs to gather information beyond what the client can or should provide for the evaluation. Therefore, MIGA has to spend resources (including travel) to gather data from clients and other stakeholders. By assuming 10 self-evaluations per year ($400,000), the self-evaluation expenditure is about one percent of the administrative budget (MIGA administrative budget of $43.9 million in FY12).

With regard to the costs of M&E relative to use of the M&E information (table 4.4), staff responded that 15 percent of new IFC investments referred to the XPSRs, and 45 percent to DOTS information. At the same time, they receive inputs from economists or DOTS champions (46 percent and 42 percent of projects, respectively), and they use M&E information extensively. Every year, around 70 self-evaluations (XPSRs) were produced with a staff time cost of $7,500 per evaluation, and 86–264 projects per year were somewhat influenced by M&E information (table 4.5).

For Advisory Services, the footprint of M&E is nearly 70 percent of new projects. The higher cost for Advisory Services M&E compared with Investment Services is because there is no alternative performance measurement matrix. Investment projects have an extensive credit and E&S data gathering and analysis system, which benefits development tracking. Also, Advisory Services is conducting many thematic and facility evaluations, partly to satisfy donors' requirements, that push its M&E costs relatively higher.

The cost-efficiency analysis is based on number of projects "reached" by M&E instruments and cost per reach. This can be interpreted as a marginal benefit

Table 4.4	Uses of M&E Instruments		
Use	IFC Investment Services	IFC Advisory Services	MIGA
Direct	XPSR = IO directly used in 15% of new projects DOTS = IO directly used in 40% of new projects	PSR = Project staff directly used 57 percent of new projects PCR = project staff directly used 67 percent of new projects	Underwriters applying learning from self-evaluation
Indirect	IO also used economists in 46% of new projects, DOTS champions in 42% of new projects Economists and DOTS champions are extensive users of XPSR and DOTS to synthesize results	Project staff also receives M&E officers' inputs. 79% of new projects M&E officers are extensive users of PSR, PCR, and other evaluations (thematic)	N/A

Source: IEG.
Note: DOTS = Development Outcome Tracking System; IO = investment officers; M&E = monitoring and evaluation; PCR = Project Completion Report; PSR = Project Supervision Report; XPSR = Extended Project Supervision Report.

Table 4.5	Influence of M&E Information		
IFC Investment Services	**IFC Advisory Services**		**MIGA**
Min: 15% of projects Max: 46% of projects had trace of M&E footprint	Min: 57%, max 79% of new projects had trace of M&E footprint		
New commitments: 576 projects in FY12 1,535 companies under supervision covered by DOTS	639 active projects 200 new projects		
M&E footprint (min: 86, max 264 new projects and 1,535 portfolio companies)	M&E footprints (min: 114, max: 158 new projects and 639 active projects)		
Project M&E covers Min 1,621 projects Max 1,799 projects That translates to $,1834 to $2,035 per project reach	Project M&E covers Min: 753 projects Max: 797 projects $13,801 to $14,608 per project reach		Unable to estimate

Source: IEG.

Note: DOTS = Development Outcome Tracking System; M&E = monitoring and evaluation.

from the M&E expenditure. For investment projects, M&E cost per project reach is between $1,834 and $2,035. For Advisory Services, the cost per project reach is between $13,800 and $14,608. This is high, but that is because M&E is the primary source of performance tracking for advisory business. For investment projects, performance monitoring is also conducted through investment portfolio review functions (CRR alone accrues total processing cost of about $17 million per year,[2] compared with the estimated total cost of $11.1 million for Advisory Services M&E).

Although the share of M&E costs in MIGA's budget is in line with or below comparators, the cost per evaluation is estimated at $40,000, because of senior staff participation in MIGA self-evaluations. The lack of periodic tracking of project performance also requires field data collection and stakeholder interviews at the time of evaluation, which has cost implications. Finally, the emphasis on learning by involving MIGA operational staff to undertake self-evaluation means that its capacity to conduct a large number of self-evaluations is constrained. This indicates a critical challenge for MIGA's evolving M&E system—to expand coverage while reducing significantly the unit cost per evaluation. This requires finding a cost-effective way of measuring the development effectiveness of MIGA projects that is consistent with MIGA's business model as a political risk insurer. As self-evaluation is mainstreamed, the unit cost is expected to decline.

The efficiency of IFC and MIGA M&E systems involves a comparison of costs and benefits. The benefits are much harder to estimate than the costs. Incremental impacts of M&E on IFC's financial returns can be viewed as a proxy for—although a highly imperfect one, and a lower bound of—the development benefits generated by IFC. The total above spending represents 2.5 percent of administrative budget for IFC and about 1 percent for MIGA. If we take the case of IFC, the M&E expenditures could be compensated by just a small increase in the average returns on investment. Thus as an illustration, the annual M&E expenses of $14 million can be recovered with only 4 bps (0.04 percent) increase in the return on average investment assets of $31.4 billion.

Is there evidence that M&E expenditures have the potential to generate incremental returns to IFC? As illustrated in previous sections, there is a correlation between identification and use of relevant lessons from experience overall SAS work quality and therefore development outcomes. But learning from M&E influences not just development outcomes but also IFC's financial returns, which are part of IFC's assessment of project outcomes. This is because M&E generates lessons that can reduce business risks and improve SAS, development, and business outcomes.

A case in point is equity. One of the key contributors to IFC's net income is the return on IFC's equity portfolio. SAS work quality is one of the important factors associated with profitable equity investments. As shown in figure 4.1, as SAS work quality improves, the chances of achieving higher equity returns increase, in particular exceptionally high equity returns. Simply put, better SAS work can improve the prospects of good equity returns by avoiding poorly performing equities or by investing in equities with better prospective returns (equity returns are also influenced by market conditions, but these are outside IFC's control). For example, average financial rate of return was 4.4 percent for equity projects with low SAS work quality. This can be compared to 17 percent for those with high SAS work quality. In sum, higher work quality contributes to 12.6 percent differences in financial rate of return for projects with equity.[3]

Figure 4.1	Distribution of Equity Return by Screening, Appraisal, and Structuring Work Quality from XPSRs

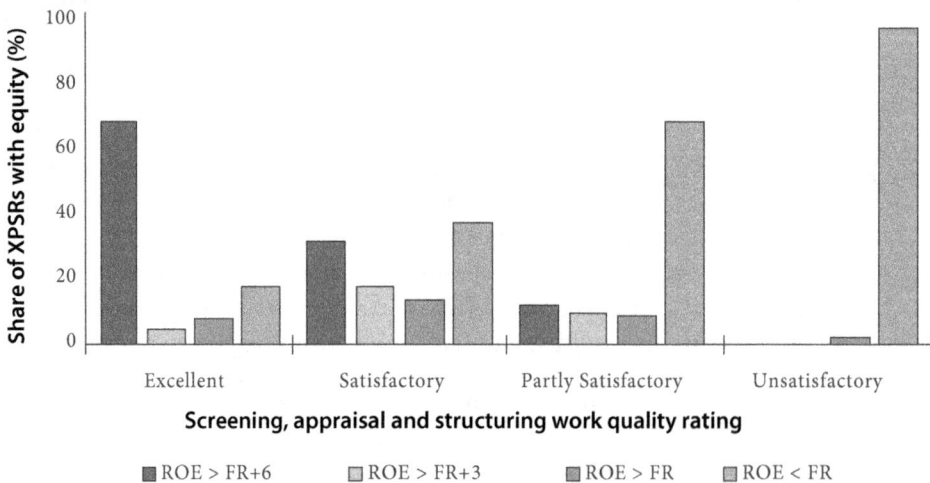

Source: IEG.
Note: All XPSR data are used; FR = fixed-rate loan equivalent, ROE = return on equity, XPSR = Expanded Project Supervision Report.

Although it seems that the potential for better work quality and knowledge derived from M&E to improve equity returns can be high, it would actually take just a small fraction of marginal improvement to compensate for M&E expenditures. Indeed, IFC's outstanding equity investments were $9.774 billion at the end of FY2012. If we assume modest improvement of SAS work quality in just 1 percent of this total equity amount from "partly unsatisfactory" to "satisfactory," the possible equity return can be enhanced by $36 million.[4] In other words, regarding efficiency, current IFC level of M&E expenditure could be more than compensated by achieving modest improvement in work quality as a result of M&E-generated lessons and information. Moreover, as indicated, these financial benefits for IFC represent just a fraction of the overall development benefits that greater effectiveness of IFC operations can entail for all relevant stakeholders.

Notes

1. Using the XPSR sample (70 XPSRs from 2008–11), a dummy variable of 0 was assigned for projects with either completely missing lessons section, lessons without specific actionable item (only portfolio description of past projects), not mentioning issues which were pointed out in the XPSR and/or EvNote, or very limited statements in the lessons section (that is, discussed only about sponsor selection issues). A dummy of 1 was assigned for all others. A regression against SAS work quality success (1 = Satisfactory or Excellent, 0 = Partly Satisfactory or Unsatisfactory) as the dependent variable. The result was statistically significant at 5 percent, indicating correlation between high SAS work quality and documenting lessons in the Project Data Sheet—Early Review document. SASWQ versus lessons is statistically significant.

2. Based on IFC budget numbers by activities.

3. Similarly, in the past, IEG estimated that the aggregated equity return was 16.4 percent for project with high work quality, while the return was -6.0 percent for those with low work quality (IEG 2006).

4. Based on the XPSR results by equity investment amount, SAS work quality rating distribution was: 20 percent "excellent", 54 percent "satisfactory", 22 percent "partly unsatisfactory" and 5 percent "unsatisfactory." The rate or return were as shown in figure 4.1, with FR = 4 percent. With IFC's outstanding equity investment amount as of end of FY12 ($9,774 million), estimated rate of return was 2.4 percent. If we assume "partly unsatisfactory" as 21 percent and "satisfactory" as 55 percent, then the rate of return became 2.8 percent. One percent represented about $36 million, which can be compared to the total M&E spending of $14 million.

References

IEG (Independent Evaluation Group). 2006. "Risk Intensity and Project Outcomes." IFC Evaluation Brief 7, World Bank, Washington, DC.

Mayne, J. 2012."Contribution Analysis: Coming of Age." *Evaluation* July 2012 18(3): 270–80.

Chapter 5

Main Findings and Recommendations

The overarching question of this evaluation is: Are the M&E systems of IFC and MIGA equipped to inform the organizations on their performance and results? IEG approached the question through three specific evaluation questions (see chapter 1). This chapter summarizes the findings for each question and puts forth actionable recommendations to improve IFC and MIGA's M&E systems.

Findings

IEG found convincing evidence that IFC and MIGA have improved their abilities to describe and measure their impacts on economic development and that overall their M&E systems are better equipped to inform decision making on development impacts. IFC in particular has a well-designed system of monitoring and self-evaluation that generates critical and reliable project information that can be aggregated. Use of the ESRD system for E&S appraisal of IFC's performance standards projects has been significant improvement from the earlier Safeguard Policy framework. MIGA is also improving its system of self-monitoring and evaluation.

To what extent does the mechanism in place ensure that M&E systems generate credible, timely, and relevant information?

For investment projects, IFC has improved its M&E system in the last three years. It increased the coverage of reach indicators from 41 percent of clients in FY08 to 80 percent in FY11. This is important because IFC uses the reach indicators in its external reporting. The new M&E systems enable IFC to record relevant M&E information throughout the project cycle. There is a system for quality checks on indicators, including the annual Quality Control Review by CDI and quality assurance review of selected indicators by external assurance.

Several aspects of the M&E system could be improved: (1) There are gaps in series tracing PSD outcomes; (2) there is evidence of a decline in XPSR quality; and (3) some M&E data used in critical applications are based on estimates or are not validated at the source.

The M&E system for IFC's Advisory Services projects is well integrated in the project cycle, with M&E officers playing important and formal roles in quality assurance. CDI assesses quality at entry, focusing on relevance of objectives, robustness of the logical framework, and appropriateness of indicators; the department also reviews PSRs with special attention to indicators and ratings. Based on IEG evaluations of 2008–10 PCRs, the gathering of baseline data and its quality need significant more improvement. During the same period, PCR quality has improved relative to several benchmarks.

Nonetheless, there are weaknesses that should be addressed: (1) standard logframes and indicators are being applied without adapting them to projects' specific characteristics or objectives; (2) IFC work quality is not assessed in the Advisory Services evaluations; and (3) timing of evaluation at project closure is not suitable for observing most project outcomes and impacts.

MIGA has been making progress in measuring the development results of its operations. MIGA has strengthened some aspects of its project monitoring. There are new activities that indicate a more active role in measuring development results. MIGA adopted a monitoring strategy in 2011 limited to tracking compliance to MIGA's E&S requirements. MIGA uses environmental and social Performance Standard and guidelines similar to IFC's. The applicable E&S requirements are explicitly stated in every MIGA Contract of Guarantee along with the E&S reports that must be submitted to MIGA. MIGA has limited staff for E&S supervision and has only recently started to visit financial intermediary projects and their subprojects to evaluate financial intermediaries' appraisal and supervision quality and the Environmental and Social Effects on the ground.

Also in 2011, MIGA introduced the DEIS to collect sector-specific indicators and six standard development impacts indicators for each project. MIGA's operational staff began pilot self-evaluations in 2010 with an emphasis on learning. IEG found that the program had been useful for staff, giving them a better understanding of projects' development impacts and knowledge of MIGA's policies and procedures. There is scope to improve the program design to increase knowledge about results and derive lessons. Also, the program's coverage is not sufficient to accurately assess MIGA's overall performance. MIGA needs to streamline self-evaluation in its system.

To what extent does M&E information support evidence-based decision making and learning?

IFC widely uses lessons from past projects in investment project selection and structuring, and poor outcomes are associated with projects that did not effectively use lessons. The learning effects of XPSRs are not fully utilized. After recent changes in the format of project documents—dropping the section on lessons—the lessons may not be adequately considered going forward. Based on a review of XPSRs, IEG has found that recognizing and acting on the lessons can improve project selection and structuring. In a sample of unsuccessful projects, some relevant lessons were overlooked in the early review process.

IFC Advisory Services has used lessons from PCRs to a greater extent since the Project Data Sheet approval document was modified to include application of lessons to project design. The impact of several reforms on quality of project design and on development effectives has yet to be determined. How well IFC designed and executed the project was associated with development effectiveness, but, unlike investment project XPSR, assessment of IFC's work quality is not covered in the PCR.

This evaluation comes when IFC has a growing focus on development results: building a shared corporate understanding of what is strengthening the results measurement systems and improving feedback into strategies and operations. IFC's new Development Goals prioritize select reach indicators of development results tracking tools for both Investment and Advisory Services to assess progress against targets, and the M&E system is integrating various tracking mechanisms (such as credit risk and environmental and social compliance) into a results management system.

IFC's results measurement system incorporate "reach indicators" that measure the number of people reached by IFC clients or the dollar benefits to particular stakeholders, regardless of IFC's investment size. The IDGs, which specify institutional targets for benefits or other tangible outcomes, are built on reach indicators. It is important to note that reach indicators relate to IFC's client activities and cannot be attributed solely to IFC. Moreover, they do not capture incremental benefits compared to the situation without IFC's intervention. Given the strong emphasis on IDGs in IFC's business decisions, there is a risk that they lead to misalignment of incentives. For example, although it is too early to evaluate any changes in behavior, staff might focus on measuring large reach numbers for IDGs rather than paying attention to delivering meaningful impact that IFC projects could bring to people and society.

Monitoring for strategies' implementation has been evolving, with greater standardization of indicators to enable aggregation of development results. Development results ratings from DOTS and CDI-assigned Advisory Services PCRs are the main indicators for development outcomes, and there is growing use of reach indictors to measure progress. IFC has generally adjusted its strategies when indicators have shown that performance was lagging. Some strategies incorporate lessons from M&E and results from external evaluations. There are some important strategic areas that do not have overarching reach or outcome indicators, such as promoting competitive markets and competitiveness. Because of growing importance of initiatives, strategies, and programmatic approaches, IFC conducted some sector and thematic evaluation to derive lessons to guide future strategic choices; but they were not conducted in a systematic way and recent introduction of evaluation policy would contribute to enhanced selectivity of sector and thematic evaluations.

Integration of Investment Services and Advisory Services has been a frequent component of strategies as articulated in the form of joint Investment and Advisory Services initiatives stated in IFC investment board reports. Advisory Services has been used to unlock market potential, enabling entry of IFC and private investments, and to enhance the sustainability and development impact of IFC investments. There are similarities in two M&E systems for Investment and Advisory Services projects. However, there are many differences that could be obstacles to sharing information and operational lessons that could be relevant for both types of activities including in linked Investment and Advisory Services. Moreover, harmonization of indicators between the two M&E systems would help close collaboration and enhance complementarities.

MIGA progressively scaled up its self-evaluation of development results from guarantee projects since FY10 and the process is now mainstreamed. A self-evaluation is performed by the senior operational staff who are also required to prepare other new projects, so it is expected that evaluation lessons will be internalized and will influence future projects and the quality of underwriting.

In a survey of MIGA staff involved with self-evaluation, more than 70 percent responded that it improved their understanding of development impacts.

What has been the impact of M&E outputs and use on project quality and development outcomes?

M&E is expected to improve IFC's investment and advisory project results. This should occur through better project designs, timely and appropriate interventions during implementation, and better strategic focus. Regression analysis based on IEG's investment project evaluations found that high front-end work that includes using lessons from evaluations mitigated high-risk elements such as sponsor risk and delivered positive development outcomes. This suggests that it is worthwhile to take risks for better results, conditional on IFC learning from its evaluative lessons—both of successes and of failures—but appropriate actions at the appraisal/screening stage should be undertaken to recognize and anticipate these risks.

M&E influences an advisory project's outcome by providing (1) a roadmap—clear objectives, baseline data, and relevant indicators—for a project to achieve its results and (2) an instrument for corrective actions during execution. Regression analysis of data for 202 advisory PCRs suggests that M&E has worked through both of these mechanisms—better design and more effective implementation have led to better outcomes.

In MIGA, self-evaluation has had its principal benefits through staff learning. But evaluation experience has also helped in updating the Underwriting Guidelines to ensure consistency and improve due diligence.

IFC spends about $14 million per year for core M&E activities, with about $8,000 per Investment project and about $9,400 per Advisory Services project. The costs of M&E per investment project are a relatively low share of project processing costs. The costs per advisory project are significantly higher, but this is because the M&E is the primary source of performance tracking for advisory business and the system is relatively new so that IFC had to invest in setting up the entire system—for investment projects, performance monitoring is also carried out through investment portfolio review functions.

Although the share of M&E costs in MIGA's budget is in line with or below comparators, the cost per evaluation is estimated at $40,000, because of senior staff participation in MIGA self-evaluations at the initial pilot stage. The lack of periodic tracking of project performance also requires field data collection and stakeholder interviews at the time of evaluation, which has cost implications. Finally, the emphasis on learning by involving MIGA operational staff to undertake self-evaluation means that its capacity to conduct a large number of self-evaluations is constrained.

Because many staff have now exposed to self-evaluation, it is anticipated that the cost per evaluation will be lower. Nevertheless, a critical challenge for MIGA's evolving M&E system—to expand coverage while reducing significantly the unit cost per evaluation—remains. This requires finding a cost-effective way of measuring the development effectiveness of MIGA projects that is consistent with MIGA's business model as a political risk insurer.

The efficiency of IFC and MIGA M&E systems involves a comparison of costs and benefits. Benefits are much harder to estimate than costs. Incremental impacts of M&E on IFC's financial returns can be viewed as a proxy for—although a highly imperfect one, and a lower bound of—the development benefits generated by IFC. The efficiency of IFC and MIGA M&E systems appears reasonable—the total spending is 2.5 percent of administrative budget for IFC and about 1 percent for MIGA. For IFC, the M&E expenditures can be supported by just a fraction of average return on investments. Also, if improvement of the SAS work quality by just a modest 1 percent of IFC's total equity amount from "partly unsatisfactory" to "satisfactory" work quality is assumed, the possible equity return can be enhanced by the amount that can easily exceed the current level of M&E spending. Therefore, current IFC level of M&E expenditure could be more than compensated for by achieving modest improvement in work quality as a result of M&E-generated lessons and information. Moreover, these financial benefits for IFC represent just a fraction of the overall development benefits that greater effectiveness of IFC operations can entail for all relevant stakeholders.

Recommendations

IFC and MIGA have increased their emphasis on measuring and assessing their contributions to economic development. Overall, their M&E systems are becoming better equipped to inform decision making for greater development impact. In the case of IFC's Investment and Advisory Services, M&E seems to be contributing to better project results by improving project design, timely and appropriate interventions during project implementation, and strengthening the strategic focus. IEG has a series of recommendations for IFC and MIGA to make further improvements.

In light of these findings, IEG has three recommendations to improve quality of M&E for Investment Services projects:

Where there are specific PSD objectives for investment projects, at least one relevant PSD indicator should be systematically tracked in the DOTS. PSD—for example, improved competition, demonstration effects of a business model, or host country sectoral transformations—is a rationale for many IFC investments. However, in the investment projects' DOTS, only a few indicators track PSD and about 46 percent of projects sampled had no such indicator. In the sample, only 28 percent of evaluated projects had DOTS indicators that were directly relevant to the expected PSD outcomes such as demonstration effects or increased competition that are critical for IFC's development mandate. There is a need for systematic reflection of expected PSD effects of IFC investment interventions, including causal chains to link IFC's activities to outcomes and indicators.

All XPSRs should be delivered on time and their quality improved through better management oversight, guidance, and clearance, plus the involvement of senior investment officers in their conduct. The quality of XPSRs has declined by three measures: (1) XPSR's rated as "good practice" dropped from 50 to 25 percent between 2007 and 2011; (2) in 2011, staff assigned higher self-ratings for development outcome and IFC work quality in 20 percent and 18 percent of XPSRs, respectively, as compared with independent assessments, and the gaps between the self and IEG ratings have been increasing in the last four years; and (3) for the first time in 2010 IFC did not complete 6 XPSRs during the program year. Possible reasons are (1) less experienced junior staff drafting self-evaluations without sufficient oversight, (2) a larger XPSR program following IFC's portfolio growth over the last five years, or (3) portfolio staff also working on new projects, which takes precedence. IEG recommends that management work to restore the quality of the XPSR program.

IFC should conduct selective tests and reviews to validate information provided by clients. For unaudited information, selective direct data verification is needed to enhance the credibility and reliability of data supplied by companies. Any assumptions and data limitations or biases should be publicly disclosed. The external assurance provider's mandate should be expanded to include assessment of the credibility and attribution of data—particularly related to IDGs—appropriate verification, and whether IFC is effectively disclosing data limitations or biases. DOTS indicators are based in part on data from audited financial reports, company annual reports, and other validated sources. However, other data are based on assumptions by client and IFC staff, and IFC does not have a process to verify data integrity other than through a desk review of information received. IFC has pioneered external assurance of its development results reporting. However, this review has been limited to a small portion of the information; only ex post MSME loan data are externally assured, that is, only 1 of 15 measures of Development Reach by IFC investment clients. Moreover, similar to IFC's CDI quality control, the assurance provider's review does not include contacting clients, visiting projects, or communicating with field-based staff. Direct data verification for some data that are based on less credible sources would enhance the credibility and reliability of data supplied by companies and staff, and any assumptions and data limitations or biases should be publicly disclosed.

Furthermore, IEG has one recommendation to make the M&E information more valuable in investment decision making and learning:

Reinforce the culture of learning lessons from IFC's previous investment projects during appraisal, design, structuring, and approval stages. Reintroducing the lessons section in appraisal documents may contribute to this. IEG recommends that the lessons learned from prior projects be used in project appraisal and structuring discussions. It would also be helpful to provide guidance for identifying lessons and reflecting lessons for meaningful discussion during the review stage. Many factors affect investment project outcomes, but evaluation results have shown that projects with poor outcomes are associated with poor upfront work quality that includes ignoring lessons. The lessons serve as a basis for defining the areas of focus during appraisal. IFC had a section in its project documentation to list the salient lessons, the section was recently dropped.

Two recommendations to improve quality of M&E system for Advisory Services follow:

Revise the standard indicators based on appropriate results chains or theory of change of business lines, strategies, and project objectives. Among PCRs completed in 2010, 90 percent fell short of using relevant standard indicators. Standard indicators in Advisory Services are not always adequate to track project results as per project objectives. In some cases, poor core indicators linked to poorly articulated objectives have led to weak impact measurement. Moreover, the increasing reliance on standard indicators that are only weakly related to project objectives could transform the self-evaluation process into a monitoring exercise focused on checking achievement of standard indicators rather than analyzing achievement of objectives and understanding the factors behind success or failure.

Address the issue of timing of IFC's Advisory Services self-evaluation system to ensure projects are sufficiently mature to more meaningfully assess their development results. In doing so, IFC might either consider conducting self-evaluation two to three years post completion, possibly on a sample of projects as done for XPSRs, or launching a postcompletion system based on clear selection criteria for projects to be included. IEG could not assign development effectiveness ratings to 18 percent of projects selected for evaluation, in most instances (65 percent of the cases) because projects had not achieved results at the time of IEG evaluation and, in 35 percent of instances, because of insufficient information and lack of credible evidence. Moreover, even among those projects for which IEG assigned development effectiveness ratings, 41 percent could not be rated at the impact level because impacts had not been achieved by evaluation/project closure or because there was insufficient information and evidence to assign a rating.

Given the limitations of the PCR instrument to adequately assess outcomes and impacts at project closure, IFC may not count on sufficient evidence to systematically evaluate completed advisory services projects and provide insights into the causal relationships between interventions and longer-term results. IFC has attempted to capture longer-term results through impact and other types of evaluations, as well as through some ad hoc postcompletion monitoring efforts. However, this has not been done in a systematic way across IFC and is largely de-linked from IFC's self-evaluation system. Since FY10, Advisory Services has revised its project objective-setting approach to determine what is achievable within the project timeframe and budget and stated that they are aiming to capture intermediate results of projects. This practice may be strengthened and supplemented by a systematic, sample-based postcompletion evaluation system aimed at capturing impacts.

Furthermore, IEG has one recommendation to make the M&E information more valuable in Advisory Services decision making and learning:

In the current process of revising PCR guidelines, IFC should include an assessment of IFC work quality in Advisory Services self-evaluations. The PCR framework does not contain a direct assessment of IFC's quality of work. The section of IFC's role and contribution usually includes some aspects of self-evaluation of IFC's role but not systematic aspects. Based on the experience from XPSRs (which includes this section), IFC would get greater learning benefits by explicitly evaluating the quality of its work—design and execution—and its relationship to other performance dimensions. IFC may consider using the work quality dimension in a revised version of the PCR Guidelines. This would help align the evaluation frameworks for Investment Services and Advisory Services.

IEG has two recommendations to make the M&E information more valuable in decision making and learning at the corporate level:

When IFC interventions involve combined Investment and Advisory Services, project M&E should more explicitly reflect results measurement of both advisory business lines and industries. IFC is increasingly combining Investment and Advisory Services to achieve development goals. Some of the lessons in Investment projects could be relevant to Advisory Services and vice versa. Although there are some common elements in the respective results measurement frameworks, there are also asymmetries.

IFC's regional, country, sector, and Advisory Services business line strategies and initiatives should contain an explicit results matrix to assess strategic objectives, with relevant indicators to track progress and evaluate in a systematic manner, preferably embedded in periodic strategy updates. IFC should pilot approaches to improve the measuring and reporting of key results on the areas of critical institutional objectives that go beyond project performance, such as private sector development and poverty reduction. Despite the growing importance of initiatives, strategies, and programmatic approaches, IFC has not systematically evaluated such strategic interventions. Most evaluations are conducted at the project level, which are not, by themselves, sufficient to measure strategic impact on sector efficiency, market functioning, competitiveness, or poverty reduction.

IEG has one recommendation to improve MIGA's M&E system:

MIGA should—

- *Streamline the project-evaluation approach and process to align more closely with MIGA's business model and conditions on data gathering.*
- *Reduce cost burden on project evaluation, possibly by strengthening periodic collection of project data in line with industry practices.*
- *Increase coverage of evaluated projects to enhance the ability to derive meaningful results at the corporate level.*

MIGA has mainstreamed self-evaluation of its guarantees and has strengthened some aspects of its project monitoring. However, the coverage of MIGA projects through self-evaluation can be strengthened to enhance the ability to assess MIGA's overall development performance. As a development institution, MIGA should be able to know the development effectiveness of its portfolio.

Appendix A

Results Frameworks for IFC and MIGA Interventions

A.1. Results Frameworks for Assessing IFC Investment and MIGA Guarantee Interventions

The International Finance Corporation (IFC) investment and the Multilateral Investment Guarantee Agency (MIGA) guarantee interventions have special characteristics, being subject to market tests. In commercial contexts, direct beneficiaries often pay for services, and the companies normally face some degree of competition. Sponsors and project companies are motivated by profitability, but development agencies' involvement generates positive externalities of the private ventures.

This is the basis of assessing the development impact of IFC investment and MIGA guarantee projects—using the stakeholder analysis framework. It involves a detailed understanding of the project environment and identifies the key actors affected by the project, as well as the magnitude of the project's impact on them. The assessment is completed by identifying counterfactuals: "What would the position of stakeholders be if the project did not exist?" Figure A.1 shows typical stakeholders in private sector projects. This framework enables a detailed assessment of stakeholders to measure performance and judge against the quantitative financial and economic performance benchmarks.

Key stakeholders are classified into four distinctive groups: the project company (financiers), other key project stakeholders, neighbors, and the private market

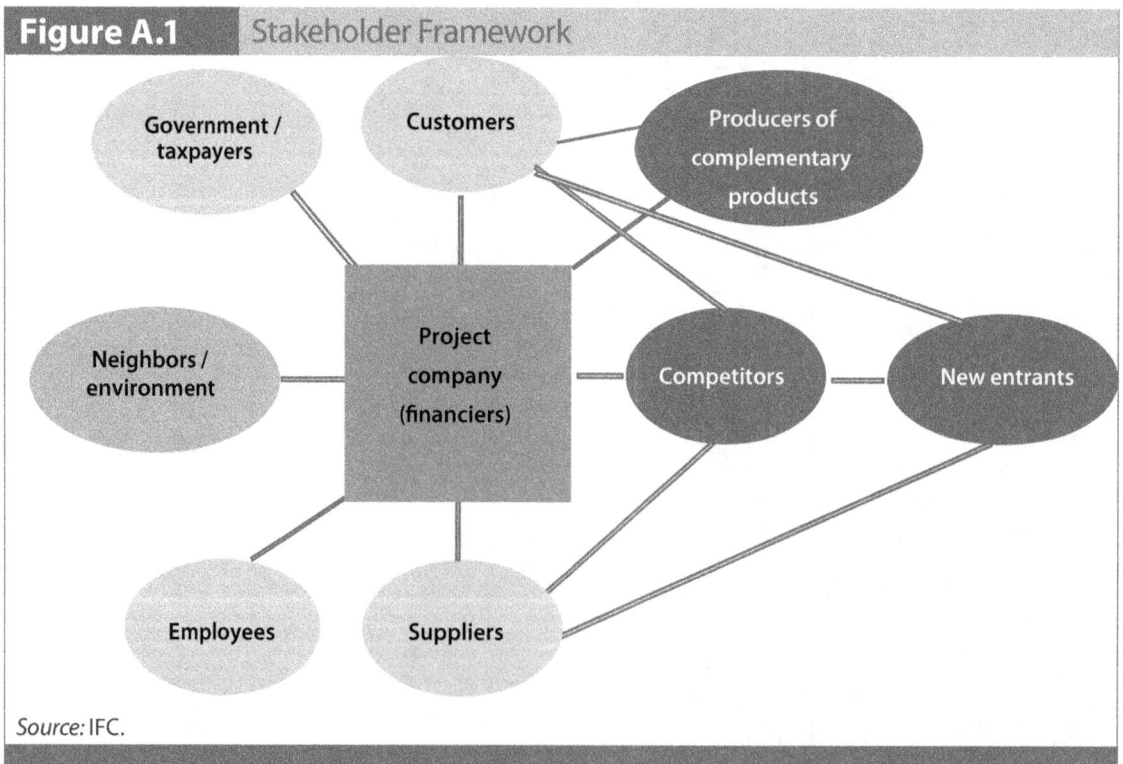

Figure A.1   Stakeholder Framework

Source: IFC.

participants beyond the project enterprises. The framework looks at the intervention's impact on each stakeholder and consolidates the effects in four different performance areas, which correspond to the four stakeholder groups: financial performance, economic performance, environmental and social (E&S) performance, and private sector development.

In financial performance, the framework looks at the impact on project financiers, particularly whether sufficient financial returns are achieved to reward the existing private investors, sustain the existing investment, and attract future investment. The other stakeholders, such as employees, customers, suppliers, and governments, are also potentially affected by the project. Assessment of such effects will illuminate the potential magnitude of net benefits to society and serve as an indicator for the economic performance of a project.

An important consideration when assessing development outcomes is the impact on neighbors, which is represented by E&S effects. Through the demonstrated effects of the projects, new entrants could be enticed to participate; this would result in increased competition and altered business practices, for example, corporate governance and regulatory systems. Such "beyond project company" effects are considered the private sector development effects.

The assessment of development effectiveness is based on the performance of the private companies that IFC and MIGA support. The framework treats the development outcomes as consequences of activities of the private companies. These could be measured by the degree of effects, both positive and negative, in not only the commercial sustainability of the company (profitability), but also in the economic, E&S, and private sector development areas. In this framework, having private business operate in a sustainable way is the fundamental requirement. This is based on the recognition that the failed business normally does not leave any positive contribution to the economy or society—if a business failed, productive investment might be wasted, jobs may disappear, tax revenues might be lost, and various other income opportunities might be gone forever.

Under this framework, projects assessed as successful in development outcome normally result in profitable businesses that make a positive contribution to the economy in terms of jobs, additional business to suppliers, benefits to consumers, and tax contributions to the government—plus there is no negative effect on the environment and the company makes positive development contributions to the private sector in general. In other words, these performance indicators indirectly illustrate progress toward the achievement of sustainable economic growth through the private sector investments, thus implicitly addressing how well the project has contributed to IFC and MIGA purposes and missions. It is important to note that this approach of recognizing development contribution is fundamentally different from the objective-based approach employed by IFC Advisory Services.

A.2. Results Framework for Assessing IFC Advisory Services Interventions

In IFC Advisory Services operations, the framework underlying assessment of the development impact of private sector operations is based on the logic model that links outcomes with project activities (see figure A.2). This is the basic building block of assessing performance that is measured against the stated objectives set at the beginning of a project. It is organized in a logic of "if, then" to connect the program's parts. By showing the logical sequences, the model describes the chain of cause and effect relationships that link project activities to intended impacts. In this way, it provides a roadmap of the program: what activities are conducted, how it is expected to work, and how desired outcomes are achieved. This model offers the benefits of systematic thinking and planning to the program design.

As with Investment Services, Advisory Services has two dimensions of criteria of merit along which IFC assesses project success: development effectiveness and institutional performance. The development effectiveness dimension has five outcome areas of assessment: strategic relevance, output achievement, outcome achievement, impact achievement, and efficiency. Institutional performance is measured through IFC's role and contribution.

Strategic relevance is considered as the retrospective fit with country priorities and conditions. It is based on appropriateness to the country's strategic objectives and conditions and appropriateness of the instrument used to meet these objectives. Output achievement measures the extent to which the tangible outputs of the project were (or were not) delivered. Outcome achievement measures changes in knowledge, behaviors, and attitudes that are a result of the intervention, to the extent that these changes can be attributed to the project. It also tracks whether there were unintended consequences of the project, and if so whether they were beneficial or harmful.

Figure A.2	IFC Advisory Services Logic Model

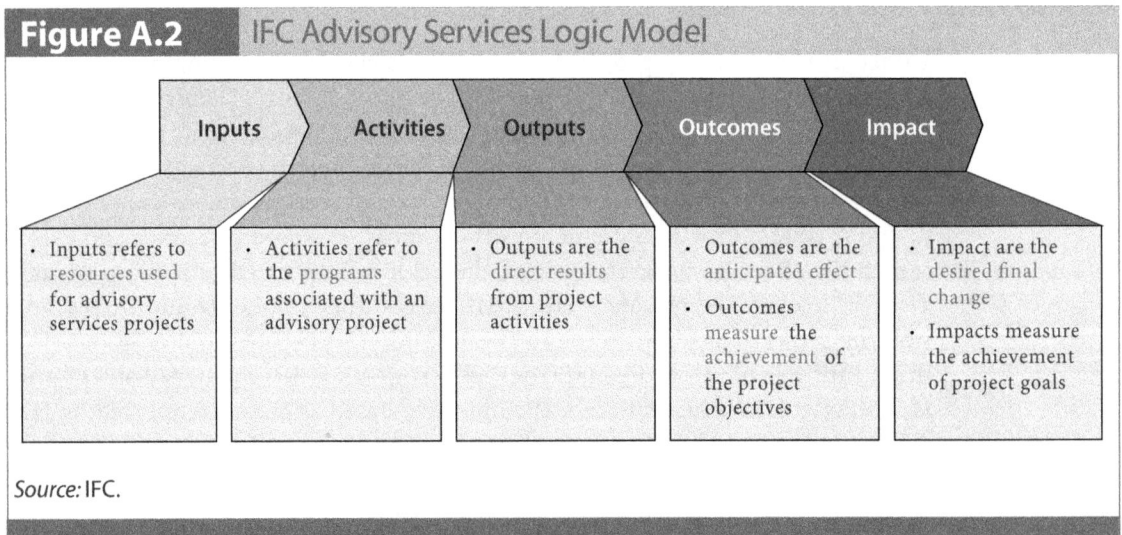

Inputs	Activities	Outputs	Outcomes	Impact
• Inputs refers to resources used for advisory services projects	• Activities refer to the programs associated with an advisory project	• Outputs are the direct results from project activities	• Outcomes are the anticipated effect • Outcomes measure the achievement of the project objectives	• Impact are the desired final change • Impacts measure the achievement of project goals

Source: IFC.

Impact achievement measures the consequences of an intervention that can be attributed to it. One way to observe this is through local replication effects, that is, intervention being replicated elsewhere, based on its demonstrated success in achieving one or more of its outcomes. As with outcome achievement, the existence of positive or negative intended and unintended consequences is also considered while assessing performance in this dimension. Finally, the efficiency outcome is essentially a cost-effectiveness outcome that assesses whether resources used for the intervention had the maximum "bang-for-the-buck," that is, whether it produced maximum results for the cost.

On the dimension of institutional performance, IFC's role and contribution measures the extent to which the intervention's objectives are unique IFC contributions relative to other participants, that is, objectives that IFC was able to achieve that other players would not have been able to achieve.

This assessment is a qualitative one, where situational descriptions and rationales provide an assessment of the achievement of objectives.

A.3. Project Evaluation Methodology for IFC Investment Operations

Introduced in 1996, the Expanded Project Supervision Report (XPSR) process first involves a self-evaluation of the project by an IFC investment department, using corporate guidelines. The self-assessment and ratings assigned by investment departments are then independently verified (or rerated) by the Independent Evaluation Group (IEG).

The *development outcome* rating is a synthesis assessment of the project's results across four development dimensions:

- *Project business success* measures the project's actual and projected financial impact on the company's financiers, that is, lenders and equity investors. The principal indicator of a project's business performance is its real, after-tax, financial rate of return.

- *Economic sustainability* evaluates the project's effects on the local economy, and the associated benefits and costs that are measured by an economic rate of return.

- *Environmental and social effects* cover (1) the project's environmental performance in meeting IFC's requirements (for example, performance standards, and relevant E&S guidelines); and (2) the project's actual environmental impacts, including pollution loads, social, cultural, and community health aspects, labor and working conditions, and workers' health and safety.

- *Private sector development impact* captures impacts beyond the project and the extent to which the project has contributed to IFC's purpose by spreading the benefits of growth of productive private enterprise.

IFC's *investment outcome* rating is an assessment of the gross profit contribution of an IFC loan and/or equity investment, that is, without taking into account transaction costs or the cost of IFC equity capital.

The assessment of *IFC work quality* involves a judgment about the overall quality of IFC's due diligence and value added at each stage of the operation:

- *Screening, appraisal, and structuring* assesses the extent to which IFC professionally executed its front-end work toward a sustainable corporate performance standard.

- *Supervision and administration* assesses the extent to which IFC has professionally executed its supervision.

- *IFC's role and contribution* measures how well IFC fulfilled its role in terms of three basic operating principles: additionality, business principle, and catalytic principle.

For each of the above dimensions, a four-point rating scale is used (excellent, satisfactory, partly unsatisfactory, and unsatisfactory), except for the synthesis development outcome rating, which involves a six-point scale (highly successful, successful, mostly successful, mostly unsuccessful, unsuccessful, and highly unsuccessful). In IEG's binary analysis, "high" refers to satisfactory or better on the four-point scale and mostly successful or better on the six-point scale.

A.4. Evaluation System for IFC Advisory Services Operations

At completion of each operation, the advisory service team provides a self-assessment of performance in a Project Completion Report (PCR). These reports are completed for all advisory services projects, unless they were dropped or terminated. IEG is responsible for the review and validation of completion reports for Advisory Services projects. Advisory Services projects are assessed by comparing the results against the stated objectives. The PCR assigns ratings for the following dimensions:

- *Strategic relevance*—Appropriateness of project given conditions, needs or problems to which it was intended to respond, alignment with country strategies, and appropriateness of instrument used.

- *Output achievement*—Immediate project deliverables (products, capital goods, services, or advice).

- *Outcome achievement*—Short- or medium-term changes resulting from the advisory project (positive or negative, intended and unintended).

- *Impact achievement*—Intended longer-term effects of the advisory intervention.

- *Efficiency*—Whether the project costs are reasonable in relation to the potential results.

These ratings are synthesized into a single development effectiveness rating, on a six-point scale from highly successful (overwhelmingly positive development results and virtually no flaws) to highly unsuccessful (negative results and no positive aspects to compensate).

Furthermore, the PCR contains a rating on IFC's role and contribution, which assesses IFC's additionality to the project.

A.5. Ex Post Project Evaluation Methodology for MIGA Projects

A standard benchmark-based methodology is used for evaluation of MIGA guarantee projects. It rates projects in three dimensions:

Development outcome aims to capture the project's overall impact on a country's economic and social development. It is evaluated across four subdimensions:

- **Business performance** measures the guarantee project's actual and projected financial impact on the project financiers—its lenders and equity investors.

- **Economic sustainability** measures whether the project has contributed to the country's development.

- **E&S effects** measures a project's performance in meeting MIGA's environmental and social requirements, as well as its actual E&S impact.

- **Private sector development impact** aims to capture the effects of the project on the development of productive private enterprise beyond the project and relates to MIGA's mandate to enhance the flow of private foreign investment to developing countries.

MIGA's effectiveness captures MIGA's work quality in assessing, underwriting, and monitoring its guarantee projects and the added value MIGA brings to the client or project. It is assessed across three subdimensions:

- **Strategic relevance** refers to the degree of consistency of the guaranteed project with the development priorities of the host country and the Bank's country strategy.

- **MIGA's role and contribution** relates to the benefits or value added that MIGA brings as a development institution. The contribution may be catalytic (in facilitating foreign direct investment in economically sound and sustainable businesses) in encouraging the development of the political risk industry or in conveying additionality.

- **MIGA's quality of assessment, underwriting, and monitoring** assesses the extent to which the project's expected development outcomes were adequately assessed, key material risks were identified and mitigated, whether MIGA's underwriting policies and guidelines were adhered to, and whether MIGA took adequate remedial action if country or project conditions changed subsequent to issuing the guarantee.

Contribution to MIGA's financial results relates to the financial contribution by MIGA of guarantee projects it underwrites (Note: This dimension is currently not rated by IEG or MIGA pending agreement on a suitable methodology).

A four-point rating scale is used: excellent, satisfactory, partly unsatisfactory, and unsatisfactory.

Appendix B

IEG Criteria for Assessing M&E Quality
for Advisory Services

Each PCR validation includes IEG's assessment of monitoring and evaluation (M&E) quality and reported in an EvNote. For each question, three different ratings are assigned: (1) great extent, (2) some extent, or (3) little or no extent.

Q1: To what extent does the PCR contain sufficient information to support a rating for this indicator?

A. Development Effectiveness
    –   Strategic relevance
    –   Output achievement
    –   Outcome achievement
    –   Impact achievement
    –   Efficiency
B. IFC's Role and Contribution

Q2: To what extent does the PCR use appropriate and monitorable indicators to support a rating (in PCR or supervision reports)?

    –   Output Achievement
    –   Outcome Achievement
    –   Impact Achievement

Q3: To what extent does the PCR—

    –   Use baseline data appropriately?
    –   Differentiate outputs, outcomes, and impacts?
    –   Discuss results of all program components?
    –   Concur with appraisal and supervision documents?
    –   Contain useful and well-structured lessons?

Q4: To what extent does the approval document—

    –   Cite relevant baseline data?
    –   Establish clear project objectives?
    –   Cite intended indicators for results tracking?

Q5: To what extent do the supervision documents—

    –   Report on up-to-date project developments?
    –   Track relevant indicators?
    –   Provide a coherent audit trail of results?

Appendix C

Electronic Survey of IFC and MIGA Staff

Five surveys were conducted between July and October 2012 to solicit opinions and comments from IFC and MIGA staff on their respective M&E systems and their use.

The IFC operational staff surveys contained questions about the actual practice of setting project objectives, the sources of information used in project preparation—during design as well as supervision. The surveys were divided into two categories: Investment and Advisory Services. Recipients of the investment staff survey are IFC staff classified as the investment job stream, with staff grade level F and above (population: 882). Recipients of the Advisory Services staff survey are IFC staff classified as the advisory job stream, with staff grade level F and above (population: 773).

The third survey targeted economists, strategists, Development Outcomes Tracking System (DOTS) champions, M&E officers, and staff in the Development Impact Department. These recipients were separated from those receiving the two surveys above, because of the more M&E-intensive nature of their roles and responsibilities in articulating a project's expected development impact, as well as identification of indicators, markets distortion effects and inefficiencies, and so forth. These recipients were asked questions about their use of various M&E information and data, for project-related or strategy-related activities (population: 104).

The fourth survey targeted environmental and social specialists. These specialists, assigned for investment businesses, were asked about sources of information used when conducting development outcome assessments for DOTS and XPSRs (population: 57).

IEG conducted a MIGA staff survey of self-evaluation pilot participants. MIGA staff who participated in at least one of the 13 past self-evaluations were invited to answer the survey (population: 38). The questions focused on the learning value from self-evaluations, the application of lessons into actual work, and experiences in data gathering and preparation of the self-evaluation report.

The email addresses of recipients of the IFC surveys were obtained from IFC human resources based on the criteria noted above. For economists, strategists, DOTS champions, M&E officers and staff in the Development Impact Department, the email distribution list for DOTS champions meetings and the list of Results Measurement Network participants were used. For the survey of environmental specialists, a detailed staff list of the Environmental and Social Department was used. For the MIGA survey, staff names listed in each self-evaluation report were used.

The exact phrasing and wording of questions and answer choices are different among the surveys, reflecting the variance in business practices between IFC Investment and Advisory Services and MIGA. These surveys were confidential and the responses have been presented in aggregate form to protect the anonymity of the participants.

To test the robustness of the survey responses, all responses were first converted to binary responses. The implied error band for each question was calculated, based on the size of the sample (number of respondents answering the question), size of population (number of survey recipients), choice of confidence interval (90 percent), and variance of the population on the question. Since this variance is difficult to measure, a worst case assumption is made across all questions, that is, all respondents are equally split for and against the question, thus maximizing variance. Implied error is thus potentially overestimated. If the error bands for the two options do not overlap, then the result is robust. Figures C.1 and C.2 show characteristics of the population that received the survey and of the respondents, for Investment Services and Advisory Services.

Figure C.1 Investment Services Respondents Characteristics, by Department

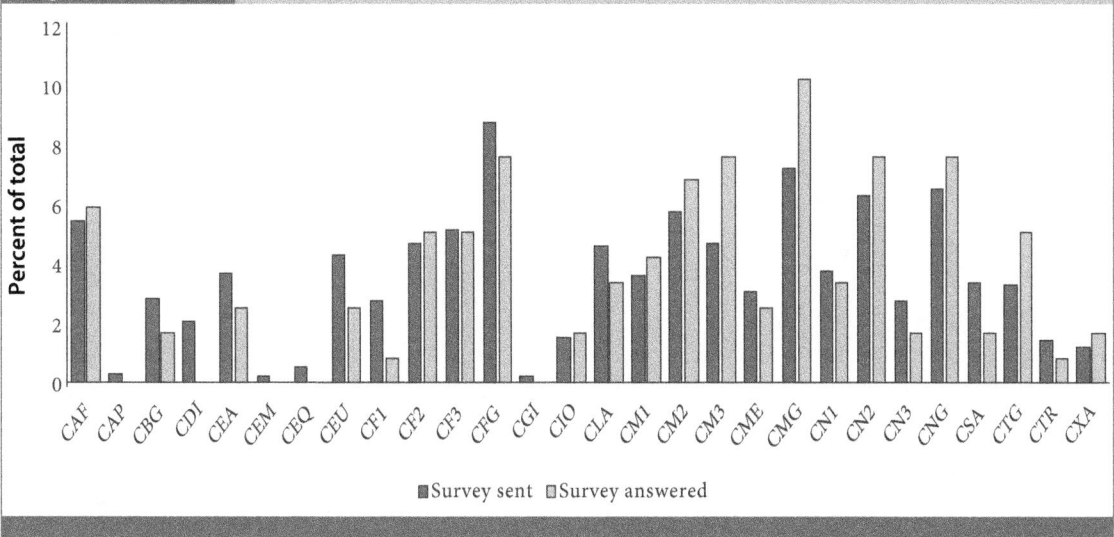

Figure C.2 Advisory Services Respondents Characteristics, by Department

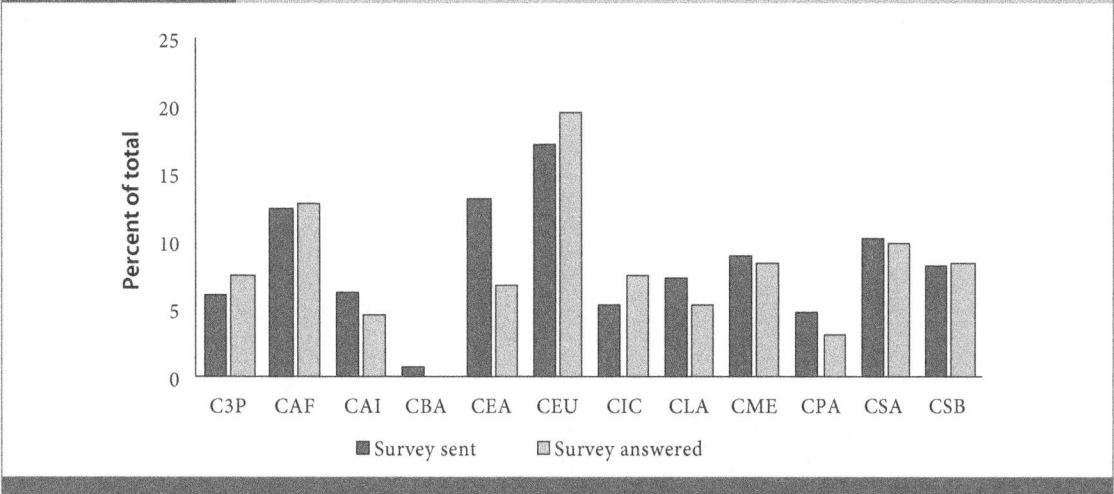

Appendix D

IFC Work Quality Assessment for
Advisory Services Projects

For validated projects, IEG reviewed project documents and assigned IFC work quality ratings for project preparation and design and project implementation.

The review assessed following areas:

Project preparation and design work quality:

- Clearly stated objectives with realistic project outcomes and impacts
- Appropriate mix of components or activities needed to achieve intended objectives
- Proper market or needs assessment
- Proper identification of project risks and proposed mitigation
- Appropriate tailoring of project and work program to country conditions
- Identification of appropriate and highly committed counterpart/partner, given the objectives
- Project design took a phase or programmatic approach (project is part of a series of combined or planed interventions in a country or sector, and interventions are properly phased)
- Promotion of local ownership of the project (that is, through creation of multiple stakeholders)
- Realistic timetables for achieving results
- Clearly designed exit strategy (project's sustainability post-IFC)
- Others as relevant.

Project implementation work quality:

- Good consultant work
- Right mix of local/international expertise
- Results-based project management
- Flexible and proactive implementation (to respond to changing local conditions)
- Proactive client engagement and follow-up
- Encouraged project's ownership by keeping local stakeholders engaged
- Effective coordination with other donors
- Adequacy to attention to sustainability (ensuring sustainable exit strategy)
- Project sufficiently staffed to effectively manage project work
- Others as relevant.

Ratings are—

- Excellent—IFC work could serve as a best-practice example with no shortcomings.

- Satisfactory—IFC work was of generally acceptable performance with no material shortfalls.

- Partly Unsatisfactory—There was a material shortfall at least in one important area.

- Unsatisfactory—There were material shortfalls in several areas *OR* a glaring mistake or omission bordering on negligence in at least one important area.

Bibliography

Haddard, L., Y. Pinto, D. Bonbright, and J. Lindstorm. 2010. "People-Centered M&E: Aligning Incentives So Agriculture Does More to Reduce Hunger." *IDS Bulletin* 41.6. Brighton: IDS.

IEG (Independent Evaluation Group). 2007. *Independent Evaluation of IFC's Development Results: Lessons and Implications from 10 Years of Experience.* Washington, DC: World Bank.

———. 2008. *Independent Evaluation of IFC's Development Results: IFC's Additionality in Supporting Private Sector Development.* Washington, DC: World Bank.

———. 2009. *Independent Evaluation of IFC's Development Results: Knowledge for Private Sector Development—Enhancing the Performance of IFC's Advisory Services.* Washington, DC: World Bank.

———. 2011. *Evaluative Lessons from World Bank Group Experience: Growth and Productivity in Agriculture and Agribusiness.* Washington, DC: World Bank.

———. 2012. *Afghanistan Country Program Evaluation.* Washington, DC: World Bank.

IFC (International Finance Corporation). 2011. *Annual Report.* Washington, DC: World Bank

———. 2012. *Annual Report.* Washington, DC: World Bank

Kingombe, C. Massa, I. and Willen te Velde, D. 2011. "Comparing Development Finance Institutions Literature Review." Overseas Development Institution, London.

MIGA (Multilateral Investment Guarantee Agency). 2011. *Annual Report.* Washington, DC: World Bank.

———. 2012. *Annual Report.* Washington, DC: World Bank.

Organisation for Economic Co-operation and Development-Development Assistance Committee. 2006. *Evaluation Systems and Use: A Working Tool for Peer Reviews and Assessments.* Paris: OECD.

———. 2011a. *Evaluating Development Co-operation Summary of key Norms and Standards,* 2nd ed. Paris: OECD.

———. 2011b. "Busan Partnership for Effective Development Co-operation." http://www.oecd.org/dataoecd/54/15/49650173.pdf.

www.ingramcontent.com/pod-product-compliance
Lightning Source LLC
Chambersburg PA
CBHW081506200326
41518CB00015B/2397